BUILDING
cities

BUILDING
cities

TOWARDS A CIVIL SOCIETY AND SUSTAINABLE ENVIRONMENT

Edited by Norman Crowe, Richard Economakis, and Michael Lykoudis

With Mark Gage, Ayako Kawashima, Stephanie Murrill, Laura Shea

SERIES ON ARCHITECTURE

UNIVERSITY OF NOTRE DAME SCHOOL OF ARCHITECTURE

ARTMEDIAPRESS

ACKNOWLEDGMENTS

The editors of *Building Cities* would like to thank all the contributors of essays and buildings and design projects who made this book possible. We are grateful for the letters of recommendation and support that were written by Léon Krier, Demetri Porphyrios, and Jorge Hernandez. Appreciation and thanks go to the faculty and students of the School of Architecture at the University of Notre Dame, as well as to the two chairpersons of the school, Thomas Gordon Smith and Carroll William Westfall, for their support and encouragement of the ongoing work for this publication. Special thanks go to Barbara Panzica and the school's staff for their patience and help in providing the logistical support for the project. Finally, we would like to thank the Graham Foundation for Advanced Studies in the Fine Arts and the members of the University of Notre Dame School of Architecture Advisory Council and its chair, Martin Knott, for their financial support.

Norman Crowe, Richard Economakis and Michael Lykoudis, Editors
Mark Gage, Ayako Kawashima, Stephanie Murrill and Laura Shea, Editorial Committee

PHOTOGRAPHIC CREDITS

Frédéric Achou pp 92, 99; © Steven Brooke Studios p 72; Sylvie Desauw pp 56 bot, 89; Carlos Domenech p 96; Duncan Stroik p 43 bot; Lasse Hedberg p 58; Hester + Hardaway p 51; Michael Lykoudis pp 54 bot, 56 top, 88 top; Scott Merrill p 50; Leigh Simpson pp 102, 103; Samir Younés pp 49 top, 54 top; Matt Wargo p 55; Charlotte Wood pp 62, 63

Front Cover: Master Plan for South Bend, Aerial View of Main Square. Design Team: Charles Beck, Michael Mesko, Michael Lykoudis, Tomas Ramirez, Lisa Schmitt. Watercolors by Sean Nohelty
Back Cover: The Effects of Good Stewardship in the City and Country, Jason Montgomery
Frontis: Tuscan Taberna Analytique. Student: Thomas Larimer; Critic: Richard Economakis

Published in Great Britain in 1999 by ARTMEDIA PRESS
Park House
140 Battersea Park Road
London SW11 4NB

ISBN: 1 902889 00 2

Printed and bound in Singapore

CONTENTS

PART I: ESSAYS

Foreword by Demetri Porphyrios — 6

Introduction to the Essays
Building Cities: Towards a Civil Society and a Sustainable
    Environment by Richard Economakis and Michael Lykoudis — 8

Permanence and Architecture by Norman Crowe — 12
The Civic Order by David Selbourne — 15
The Nature and Justice of Cities by Carroll William Westfall — 20
The City of Justice by Peter Murphy — 24
Of Two Freedoms, the Political and the Artistic by Samir Younés — 26
The City, the Engineer, and the Architect by Alan Baxter — 30
Modernism and the Separated Self by Louis Sass — 34
Contemporary Perspectives by Léon Krier — 40

PART II: PROJECTS

Introduction to the Projects
From the Art of Building to the City by Norman Crowe
    and Michael Lykoudis — 42

Tectonics and Technical Issues
Information Booth — 43
Villa Indiana — 43
The Art of Proper Building — 44
Visitors' Center and Museum for Mayan Artifacts, Guatemala — 44
Doric and Ionic Analytique — 45
The Walls, Openings, and Roof for a Dovecote — 45
Archives Building for the University of Notre Dame — 46
Doric Order Analytique — 46
The Relationship Between the Natural, the Rustic,
    and the Vernacular — 47
A Parallel of Building Types — 48
US Capitol Cornerstone, Washington, DC — 49
Tectonic Models — 49

Private Buildings
Residential Types, Windsor, Florida — 50
Townhouse in Houston — 51
Apartment House in Chicago — 52
Zanitsch Residence, Deep Creek, Maryland — 54
Residence, South Bend, Indiana — 54
Riggs National Bank Branch Offices — 55
Habitat for Humanity House and Studio — 56
Residence on Rue de Laeken, Brussels — 56
Townhouse in Chicago — 57
5 Kongens Gate, Oslo — 58
Commercial Building, Birmingham, England — 59
Hotel on Cooper Square, New York — 60

Public Buildings
A Public Room: Design for a Lobby — 61
Longwall Quadrangle, Magdalen College, Oxford — 62
Court and Garden Project for a Public Building — 64
Public Library — 65
Municipal Archives Building in Nappannee, Indiana — 65
Visitors' Center and Museum for Mayan Artifacts, Guatemala — 66
A New Public Library in Madison — 66
A New Public Library — 67
Meigs Field Airport Terminal, Chicago — 68

New School in Harlem, New York — 71
Windsor Town Center, Windsor, Florida — 72
National Equestrian Center in Washington, DC — 73
Cultural Center in Kyoto — 74
Cultural Center in Bukhara — 75
Cultural Center in Isfahan — 77
Student Union at De Paul University, Chicago — 78
Minor League Baseball Stadium in Marshall, Michigan — 78
Architectural Center in Paris — 79
Aula in Rome — 79
Market Building at Paternoster Square, London — 80
Theater and Square in South Bend, Indiana — 80
National Genealogy Center in Ellis Island, New York — 81
The Pineapple Express: A Railway Station for Stewart, Florida — 82

Sacred Buildings
A Parallel of Two Sacred Precincts:
    The Stupa at Sanchi and the Agora at Athens — 83
American–Chinese Christian Disciple Center in New York — 84
Catholic Church and School in Indianapolis — 84
Mosque in Washington, DC — 85
Hall Church and Baptistery in Sauvie Island, Oregon — 86

Blocks and Streets
Redevelopment of Capitol Avenue, Washington, DC — 87
Reconstruction of the Borgo Vaticano in Rome — 87
Richmond Riverside, Richmond on Thames, England — 88
Roosevelt Road, Chicago — 88
Reconstruction of Rue de Laeken, Brussels — 89
Center for Cultural and Religious Studies in Miyajima, Japan — 90
Poundbury, Dorchester, England — 91
Le Plessis Robinson Housing, Paris — 92

Public Spaces and Monuments
Bridge Between Greece and Turkey — 93
Upper Market Monument in Augusta, Georgia — 93
Monument to Joseph Beck in Luxemburg — 94
Design for a National Garden in Washington, DC — 95
Brickell Avenue Bridge in Miami — 96
Cemetery for the City of Rome — 96
Three Proposals for the City of Rome — 97

Quarters and Neighborhoods
Reconstruction of Beirut — 98
Bruay-la-Buissière:
    Urban Restructuring of the Town of Nouveau Monde — 99
Center for Classical Studies in Nisyros, Greece — 100
Master Plan Competition, Plainfield, Illinois — 101
Channahon Town Center Competition — 101

Cities, Towns, and Villages
Pitiousa, Spetses, Greece — 102
Master Plan for Nauplion, Greece — 104
Haymount — 105
New Olympia Town Plan:
    A Proposal for a Permanent Site for Olympian Games — 105
Master Plan and Urban Design for South Bend, Indiana — 106

EPILOGUE

A Most Formidable Task by Samir Younés — 108

FOREWORD
Demetri Porphyrios

The question of how to approach the classical has been around for well over two millennia, and shows no signs of going away. The geography of the classical is more than a place of residence. It reaches across cultures and time and requires the conscientious recovery of working traditions.

Today the traditions which are relevant and must be recovered are precisely those which prise open the contradictions of modern industrial society, thereby imparting to the classical a critical dimension. The observations that follow highlight exactly these traditions which are arguably indispensable to humanist architecture and culture.

BUILDING AND ARCHITECTURE

Buildings spring from two sources. They exist and continue to be built because they fulfill two of mankind's most fundamental needs, namely shelter and civic life.

When we say that buildings provide shelter we mean exactly that: they stand solidly and defy gravity; they shed water; they provide warmth, shade, and coolness. They also provide privacy. The skills required for the production of shelter are what is known as *firmness*.

Buildings also provide comfort in the sense that they foster the use and activities for which they were intended. This is achieved through spatial composition and the careful balance between private and public activities. The house, the office, the shop, the library, the theater, the church, are all spatial arrangements which fulfill commodiously the functional and social requirements of their intended program. The skills required in fulfilling the functional and social requirements of a building are known as *commodity*.

But what distinguishes a shed from a temple is the power the temple possesses: the power to transgress the contingent reality of *firmness* and *commodity* by raising construction and shelter to the realm of the *symbol*. The artifice of constructing this fictitious (social) world through which the real is redeemed is what is known as *delight*.

ARCHITECTURE AND THE CITY

Humans are characteristically political animals. In other words our lives, aspirations, dreams, and mythical perceptions are all formed and re-formed in the context of civic debate. Buildings and architecture participate in such a civic debate as they establish functional and symbolic hierarchies between themselves and the public spaces which at the same time unite and distinguish them.

This pattern of relationships (both physical and social) between buildings and public open spaces is what constitutes the city. It is of great importance, therefore, to remember that architecture and the city are two faces of the same coin. We cannot address the one without reference to the other. In fact, I may even venture here to say that the ethical content in architecture lies exactly in the way by which the city mollifies and tempers the antagonism between the *individual* and the *community* by providing a careful balance of public and private spaces and buildings as the physical framework for the life of its citizens.

INTEGRATION OF THE BUILDING PROFESSIONS

The production of buildings has, progressively in our century, entered the cycle of commodification. The exchange value of buildings has overshadowed their use and civic values. The great majority of buildings today are built with the view to being marketed and must respond to ephemeral market forces.

As a consequence, professional expertise has been fragmented between many building professions. The gap between architect, planner, mason, structural engineer, services engineer, joiner, estimator, interior decorator, landscape designer, etc, is today not simply a matter of specialized expertise but of different philosophies, world views, aims, and aspirations. All have different agendas. It is important, therefore, that the different branches of the building industry are brought closer together so that we may share common values and understand each other's preoccupations.

In the course of the last two centuries we, as architects, have witnessed the steady decimation of our household. Out of laziness or embarrassment we have surrendered our constructional and craft skills and marginalized ourselves in the dubious world of aesthetic intellectualism. As architects we must reclaim the expertise of the mason and structural engineer, of the landscape designer and interior decorator, of the city builder and urbanist.

HANDS-ON EXPERIENCE

This interest in the integration of the building professions and trades points to another related interest, namely that of 'hands-on' experience: in other words, learning by example, familiarizing ourselves and the student with the skills and preoccupations of the different trades and professions and with the process of building.

I should hasten to clarify here that we must avoid the fetishism of craft-schools, where building a brick wall or constructing a timber truss is mistaken for 'hands-on' experience. 'Hands-on' experience can be gained only through systematic involvement in professional multi-disciplinary workshops and practices where the full spectrum of the contradictions of the building industry can become apparent.

TECHNOLOGY

That brings me to the question of technology. Technology today is commodified. The commodity of a technological product is 'what a product is there for'. In the case of the radiator it is warmth; with a telephone it is communication; a car provides transportation; a stereo furnishes music.

Technology today makes no demands on our skills, knowledge, or mythical imagination. I often wonder why people gather around a fireplace; you can read the answer in their faces glowing with excitement. But I have yet to come across a family gathered around a radiator. As technology pro-liferates, its machinery becomes more and more concealed. The more high-tech the technology, the more concealed the machinery and, in fact, the less our involvement with it.

When technological products become mere commodi-ties they deny our engagement with their machinery and technology, which leads to human estrangement (eg, think of a prefabricated wall, a suspended ceiling, high-tech ser-vices engineering, doors or windows without handles). I remember when, fresh out of Princeton, I worked with Alvar Aalto. Technology, he used to say, is true technology only when it is domesticated, when it becomes a skill and when we feel at home with it.

'Feeling at home with it' means physical engagement – which is not simply physical contact but the experience of the world through the manifold sensibility of the body. It is important that we question modern technology with the view to sharpen once again human sensibility which is strengthened through skill, because skill is nothing else but intensive and refined engagement with the world. And skill is ultimately bound up with social engagement and civic values.

TRADITION

This brings me to my final point: that of tradition. By tradition I do not mean the docile transmission of some dead deposit but rather the living repetition that manages to suggest a fresh truth. There is no such thing as a tradition that exists of its own accord. Instead, and always, tradition has to be embraced and cultivated.

In fact, the very idea of education itself hinges on tradition. For even though the teacher loses his authority when the pupil matures and forms his own insights, this passage into maturity does *not* mean that a person has repudiated tradition. On the contrary, he has made tradition his own. It is precisely in this passage into maturity that the wonder of education lies. Education exists only when tradition is freely taken over.

Today we must consider architecture in terms of its actual production. What is the tradition and nature of our building materials and how should we put together our buildings and cities? I fear that we have surrounded our-selves with a culture of debris. In fact, we are slowly coming to the conclusion that the industrial transformation of natural materials may well be responsible for the ecological imbalance we have triggered.

It is in this context that the classical is again relevant today. The classical is not about fluted shafts or polychrome pediments, because 'classicism is not a style'. Classicism is not a doctrine; it is a philosophy of life. It is the philosophy of free will nurtured by tradition. What the classical claims is that there is and ought to be a balance between nature and man. Should we forgo this balance our species will become extinct. From an ethical point of view, the classical also underlines the importance of modesty. It is not merely a mat-ter of social modesty that I have in mind, but ultimately of being modest in our relation to the universe, to the natural world and, beyond that, to that which we call sacred.

Let us temper our prejudices and reach across cultures and time so that we may heal the estrangement that humanity now constantly faces.

A version of this text was first delivered on 21 March 1997 by Dr Demetri Porphyrios as the Convocation Address on the occasion of the dedication of the Bond Hall of Architecture at the University of Notre Dame, Indiana. Copyright Demetri Porphyrios.

BUILDING CITIES
Towards a Civil Society and a Sustainable Environment
Richard Economakis and Michael Lykoudis

'The global destruction of cities and countryside, of human cultures and nature itself, can only be reversed by a global philosophical, technical, cultural, moral, and economic project: by an ecological project.' *Léon Krier*

At the threshold of the new millennium, architecture is hard pressed to show its unity of purpose. Like the god Janus, it looks in two directions at once, torn between modernism's ever-polished, steel-clad visions of a brave new world, and the determined calls for urban reconstruction and the re-establishment of cultural continuity. On one side, we have a mainstream attitude of maximal, opportunistic sub-urban growth driven by the promise of unconditional, personalized technological application and expressionistic freedom. On the other, a new traditional architecture and urbanism which measures growth and professional maturity primarily in terms of the architect's contribution toward the enhancement of a shared civil life, and which requires an enduring sense of place and urban and cultural continuity, as well as an awareness that technology should contribute toward, rather than dominate, the architectural process. This last position, after decades of steady development, has come eloquently to the fore as a convincing alternative to modernism.

The aims of the new traditional architecture are at once urban, social, and environmental. The age-old city of limits is understood to be the best model for human settlement, able to achieve a natural balance, as an equal and opposite, to the countryside from which its citizens derive their sustenance. Such a city consists of clear, delineable public and private realms which combine to form a system of contained pedestrian urban quarters of mixed use, equipped with the necessary civic, commercial, and residential apparatus of neighborhood. As Léon Krier has argued for more than twenty years, the terrible post-war tendency toward urban sprawl can only be reversed by the re-urbanization of peripheral areas and the creation of finite and distinct new urban quarters. The optimal size of these 'cities within cities' can be calculated to be approximately thirty-three hectares – ie fifteen thousand inhabitants, ie a ten-minute walk from end to end – guaranteeing proximity and accessibility of functions for the greatest possible cross-section of society. The broader metropolitan infrastructure, including public transit and vehicular corridors, light industry, and public services in general, can thus be situated appropriately in the interstitial fabric that separates the quarters.

Traditional architecture articulates the diverse constituent elements of the city by way of formal 'languages' that obviate their origins in the craft of assembling locally available natural materials of such size and weight as can be shaped and maneuvered by the human hand. The responsible architect conceives his or her buildings in full knowledge of the destructive environmental effects and long-term consequences of using industrial products and techniques. In the public domain where a universality of values is most appropriately conveyed, regional craft traditions are translated into forms of such refinement and permanence as would elevate the building to the level of civil art – architecture that, despite its distinguishing cultural accoutrements, transcends present social and practical concerns and projects itself through time and space.

The traditional city always measures itself against the human scale and enriches the urban context through a broad typological variety and clear formal hierarchies that place the public edifices and spaces in clear juxtaposition with the greater urban fabric for the benefit of the citizen. Sustainability is understood not as the tenuous framework, applied by modernist practitioners, of continual reinvestment in 'better' or 'safer' solutions of short-term effect, but rather as a universal outlook that fully harmonizes the processes of nature and artifice. The sustainable city is made up of forms that harmonize with and tolerate the specific architectural expressions of previous generations. Urban growth is projected in the context of a continuous evolution over the centuries, in which buildings remain grounded in the notions of firmness, commodity, and delight, as well as continuity and tradition. The architecture of the sustainable city is understood always as maintaining and improving itself on the basis, and for the benefit, of the common public good. As such it relies on a civil, or political, disposition of the citizens it is intended to serve. Thus the architecture of the sustainable city seeks to encourage the most direct and effective participation of all the inhabitants.

The growing success of the new traditional architecture is most appreciable in the impressive numbers of executed works and the emergence of a host of supportive professional and academic institutions. For the first time in half a century traditional buildings and towns are being constructed around the world, with increasing support and appreciation from a public eager to reinvest in a balanced co-existence with nature and the city. The movement's strength can also be gaged in the influence it has begun to have on members of the professional establishment. One need only consider the recent shift away from orthodox modernist ideology with regard to the city by Richard Rogers, the architect of hi-tech buildings such as Lloyd's in London and the Beaubourg Pompidou Center in Paris, who now urges the professional world to accept the traditional urban model as superior.

But while, wittingly or not, this revised modernist discourse echoes the decades-old argumentation of contemporary traditional architects, it ultimately fails to adapt itself to the pressing requirements of urban sustainability. For though it is meant to conjure up vibrant metropolitan settings, it is made of wasteful, polluting, and otherwise anti-ecological industrial products and techniques, and in accordance with a dissociative modernist aesthetic, neither of which can, in *talis extremis*, contribute to the creation of sound urban environments.

The traditional architect takes issue not just with modernism's cynical view of tradition and its superficial 'techno-fix' environmentalism, but more generally with its uncritical alignment with a rampant consumerist ideology. For all the earnestness of modernism's original social intentions, it has shown itself incapable of constructing a humane, genuinely sustainable environment; its grounding in zeitgeist ('spirit of the age') theory, according to which architecture must reflect the changes rather than the continuity of the present

day, restricts it necessarily to short-term policies that promote a non-committal attitude toward human settlement and the nature of the built environment.

Certainly the recent shift toward a more urban attitude by some modernist architects can be seen as a step in the right direction. At the same time it is important for the profession to understand that the global destruction of cities and countryside will not be halted merely through a new urban densification and the mechanical replication of traditional urban patterns in 'contemporary' architectural, or formal, terms. Change must involve a reappraisal of the broader socio-economic and cultural framework within which architecture and urbanism necessarily occur.

We must, however, consider the other face of Janus. It would have been hard to imagine, just ten years ago, that we would be even half as critically disposed at the close of the twentieth century. Students of architecture can choose to develop traditional schemes without being challenged as being unrepresentative of attitudes within the profession. Of those architects who choose to build according to traditional principles, the greater part do so out of deeply rooted convictions and beliefs that go far beyond the superficialities of 'style' or professional opportunism.

Having outlined and understood the essential physical and political constitution of the new sustainable city, or contemporary civil polity, traditional architects are striving to achieve the integration of functions necessary for the city's livelihood. Often they have had to operate against the most adverse and inflexible legislation, educating local planning officials and municipal authorities as to the virtues of the traditional urban model and convincing the developer of its long-term benefits. Codification of architectural and urban priorities has been applied with success by new urbanists such as Andrés Duany and Elizabeth Plater-Zyberk at developments such as Seaside, Windsor, and Kentlands.

Similar success has been achieved with regard to the reclamation of existing, blighted urbs and sub-urbs and the construction of new urban extensions: it is indeed difficult to find fault with the extension to the town of Spetses in Greece by Porphyrios Associates, the Rue de Laeken intervention in Brussels by Atelier Atlante, the new town of Port Grimaud by François Spoerry, and the Plessis-Robinson neighborhood by Nada and Marc Breitman. Tagliaventi Associates' proposal for the Marsham Street re-urbanization in London would bring to the area a much needed integration of commercial, residential, and governmental functions. Other exemplary new buildings and projects such as Piotr Choynowski's urban interventions in Oslo, John Simpson & Partners' Lime Street building in London, Quinlan Terry's Richmond Riverside development in London, and John Blatteau's Riggs Bank buildings in Maryland and Washington, DC, provide evidence of a radical shift in the architectural profession's direction which involves more than architectural and urban strategies; indeed, it assumes a political significance.

Even in the world of architectural publishing, which still caters mostly to modernist practitioners, the signs of a renewed professional sensitization to the idea of urban sustainablility, and hence to traditional architectural and urban principles, are unmistakable. Architectural bookshops now carry publications that would not have sold profitably ten years ago, including reprints of Jane Jacobs' seminal book *The Death and Life of Great American Cities*, first published in 1961, and Louis Chevalier's *The Assassination of Paris* from 1977. There is Philip Langdon's *A Better Place to Live*, James Howard Kunstler's *The Geography of Nowhere* and his more recent *Home from Nowhere*, Peter Katz's *The New Urbanism*, Norman Crowe's *Nature and the Idea of a Man-Made World*, and Peter Calthorpe's *The Next American Metropolis*, to list only a few published since 1993.

The idea of urban reconstruction as part of a global cultural and ecological project has been echoed by members of almost every discipline and science, for whom reconstruction is understood as necessarily involving the nature of the built environment. Global tendencies toward social disaggregation, alienation, 'inner city' depression and violence, economic and racial segregation, and, more generally, the abandonment of a civil ethos, have grown conspicuously against a backdrop of urban decay and dissolution. As a counterpoint to the divisive zoning attitudes, near-sighted

environmentalism, cultural relativism and formal provocationalism (shock value as an aesthetic qualification) of the architectural mainstream, the polite nature and quiet optimism of the new traditional architecture and urbanism have increasingly attracted even the most architecturally impartial or disinclined members of other disciplines.

In *Building Cities*, architects and others from outside the profession openly challenge the current state of architecture. Architect Demetri Porphyrios sets buildings in their rightful relationship to the art of building, without which humane cities are impossible. Thus he stresses the instrumentality of architecture in the creation of a healthy civil environment; the importance of engaging technology 'with a view to sharpen once again human sensibility that is strengthened in skill'; and, finally, the understanding of classicism not as a doctrine, but as a 'philosophy of free will nurtured by tradition'.

Urbanist Léon Krier extends the discussion to the issue of contemporaneity. In its fundamental grounding in the art of building, he argues, the traditional architectural and urban model will remain pertinent and adaptable, and therefore wholly modern. 'Modernity and modernism are clearly distinct phenomena and can no longer be confused or amalgamated', he explains, adding that 'it is not history and age but structure and ideas which confer quality to an urban context'. He concludes by saying that the body of knowledge necessary for the building of cities is once again fully known to us; the application of this knowledge is a reflection of civil responsibility, and a genuine interest in an architecture 'of the age'.

In 'Of Two Freedoms', architect and theorist Samir Younés draws a distinction between political and artistic freedoms, demonstrating that both politics and art are harmed if individual meanings and freedoms come to be accepted as the opposites of collective meanings and freedoms. Thus, a democratic society's encouragement of pluralism should not be confused with random permissiveness. Younés posits that artistic freedom is inseparable from three categories: the individual's intellectual freedom, the larger cultural conventions known as the *sensus communis*, and the proper realm accorded to each art.

Political philosopher David Selbourne shows us that the patterns of social and cultural decay have emerged from the corruption of a post-war liberal order. The failure of civil society, he argues, has been caused in part by the collapse of what he terms the 'principle of duty', once cultivated by the individual and understood as essential to social belonging and commitment.

But while pursuing reconstruction we must continue to seek the causes of the collapse of the traditional city in more than political and urbanistic terms; for ours is an age of unprecedented social and cultural fatalism, shaped in the grim assembly lines of industrial production and the cold-war threat of total annihilation. The civil disaggregation deplored by Selbourne not only parallels but encourages symptoms akin to schizophrenia in our treatment and understanding of the creative impulse.

This is made clear by clinical psychologist Louis Sass, who analyzes the negativism and anti-traditionalism of modernism, 'its rage for chaos', its irony and detachment, its interiorizing trends, and the alienation it fosters. Though treating the subject of literary and artistic expression, his analysis pertains equally to modernist architecture, where the 'abdication of the public self' has been prevalent since the formation the Bauhaus.

Architectural historian and theorist Carroll William Westfall reminds us that a mere collection of well-crafted and beautifully designed buildings does not necessarily a city make, thus emphasizing that architecture and urban design must ultimately be conceived in such a way as to support and enhance a just society as pertaining to the always unique exigencies of the unfolding present. Westfall speaks of '. . . the product of maturity won through experience nurtured by private reflection and public discussion among people of good will . . .'; Christian Langlois' French Senate Buildings in Paris and Porphyrios Associates' New Longwall Quadrangle at Magdalen College in Oxford stand out amongst a host of new, convincing examples of such maturity.

Structural engineer Alan Baxter explains why an architecture of community and cultural and material transcendence is just as valid and necessary today as it was sixty years ago. Proximity of functions and inclusivity are, he stresses, essential ingredients in the creation of cities and urban quarters. Projects such as Manuel Manzano-Monis' completion of the town of Fuenterrabia and the Bruay-la-Buissière town extension by Marc and Nada Breitman show how these concerns can shape real cities and neighborhoods.

Treating the subject of permanence in architecture, architect and academic Norman Crowe warns that 'our break with the tradition of permanence . . . disregards the role of architecture as a means to stability through the reinforcement of an effective and sustaining sense of place'. He argues that our understanding of and commitment to a genuine sustainability of cities and nature is reflected firstly in the way by which we build. Traditional long-term planning, Crowe maintains, 'provides a realistic time-frame for things and places that we hold as important'.

In the book's epilogue, architect and theorist Samir Younés admonishes that while the knowledge for the construction of the new sustainable city has been recovered, and while the city is beginning to be built again, a major obstacle presents itself toward its full and welcome realization. This obstacle is the all-pervasive usurpation of socio-cultural productions by technological forces with determinism of their own. The next step in an ongoing project to build a humane society, the author urges, must be to see the world from a perspective that is not framed by technological determinism.

Taken together, the essays in *Building Cities* point not only to a multi-disciplinary concurrence on positions long held by traditional architects and urbanists; they also testify to the existence of a body of knowledge and a genuine commitment by members of diverse professions who can, if allowed to work together, pave the way for a new civil culture.

The public realm sketched out by the essayists is given life through the projected and theoretical works of an army of younger architects and urbanists whose passion for their work and professional commitment promises to carry the struggle to reclaim the public realm, and the art of building cities, safely into the new millennium.

PERMANENCE AND ARCHITECTURE
Norman Crowe

A recent celebration – the dedication of the renovated Bond Hall of Architecture at the University of Notre Dame – was a poignant reminder that university campuses are among the last bastions for the once prevailing notion that buildings ought to be built to last. The more usual practice today is to assume that a building, a bridge, or a landscape soon outlives its usefulness, and that therefore it is unrealistic to use durable, expensive materials and constructional techniques designed to outlast the specific functions a building is intended to accommodate. Of course our economic system is largely based on the promotion of change as central to economic vitality, but even in circumstances when change is not necessarily warranted, the established practice of building temporary structures nonetheless necessitates periodic demolition and rebuilding. Planned obsolescence in building construction and design is one of many now-familiar species of the contemporary self-fulfilling prophecy.

In 1993 science writers for The World Watch Institute pointed out, in an article entitled 'Building Better Buildings', that St Alban's Abbey in England was built of bricks salvaged from the ruins of a Roman building put up 900 years before. Today, St Alban's is itself 900 years old. In other words, the bricks used in its construction were manufactured 1,800 years ago. To look at it another way, the resources expended for the manufacture of those bricks – the wood that fired the kilns for baking raw clay into stable bricks – has had 1,800 years to re-grow; and because the clay was extracted from the earth 900 years before St Alban's was built, the abbey's eleventh-century builders did not have to dig much new clay out of the earth.

The Institute's writers used this example to introduce a discussion about certain approaches to building construction that are far more efficient in the long run than today's normative practices – especially here in North America – practices that tend to promote demolition and reconstruction every thirty to forty years or so. The World Watch Institute report went on to estimate the resources required to mine the iron ore and bauxite and subsequently transform them into steel and aluminum using traditional manufacturing processes, as well as the pollution this operation generated. They then compared this to the extent of disturbance to the earth's surface involved in procuring clay for brick, or raw stone for masonry construction, in addition to the energy resources expended in preparing brick and stone for use as building materials. In this comparison, as one would expect, brick and stone emerged way ahead of the other materials on all fronts when viewed from the perspective of long-term economy of resource consumption and energy expenditure, as well as with respect to the generation of airborne and waterborne pollutants during the manufacturing and constructional processes and the transportation of raw and manufactured materials from procurement site to manufacturing and building sites. It is only when viewed from the standpoint of short-term economic return that steel, aluminum, and various other complex manufactured materials come out ahead. This is to say that someone's economic gain today is being accepted as more important than society's much greater loss in the future.

These economic projections, of course, work at the scale of traditional buildings, and only nominally for taller buildings, where a steel frame is necessary to support a curtain-wall and where a lightweight curtain-wall is necessary to reduce overall weight on the structural frame. But high-rise buildings notwithstanding, the predominant building type across the world is still traditional in scale (if not in character and materials), and I believe that it can be argued that the necessity for high-rise construction becomes even more questionable when we consider the high energy costs and relative impermanence of its materials and constructional processes.

In the late 1980s the National Audubon Society began to plan for the establishment of its new national headquarters. Croxton of New York was selected as the architect. As a major institution established to promote the preservation of the natural environment, Audubon was of course very much aware that its architectural decisions had to reflect its broader environmental concerns. Conventional wisdom would expect it to flee to the countryside where it could build an energy-conscious something-or-other, perhaps mostly underground and certainly well out of sight of the city. But to do so, Audubon realized, would necessitate highways for employee commutes, an unnecessary and excessive wastage of land, and the expenditure of more resources than a buried new building in the countryside could ever recover; and it recognized as well that building anew would (in effect) constitute the needless duplication in size and spatial arrangement of any one of numerous existing buildings somewhere within the core of an established, serviceable city. So Audubon's solution was to acquire and remodel an abandoned 1891 Richardsonian Romanesque building in Manhattan for its headquarters, while introducing new insulation, multiple glazing, daylighting technology, waste recovery systems, etc – all built into the old stone building fabric. An existing building thus received new life and a traditional urban enclave was enhanced at the same time, thereby avoiding contributing to the outward sprawl that now characterizes most new development.

Recently I began a study of successful local examples of traditional urbanism in the hope of demonstrating that America's traditional neighborhoods are not a thing of the past. With two graduate students I focused on a particular Chicago neighborhood that is comprised primarily of row houses, interspersed with an effective mix of shops, restaurants, bars, commercial establishments with residential housing above the street level, and various institutions including a branch library, several schools, an urban university, and a nationally known hospital. We expect the results to reveal in a convincing way the advantages of both mixed-use planning for residential neighborhoods and, especially, the effectiveness of the traditional row house with its permanent masonry facade and masonry party walls that serve as bearing walls to support the floors and roof.

Part of the row house's effectiveness has to do with its adaptability; the traditional row house maintains a clear span from one party wall to the other, thereby providing an interior that is infinitely remodelable – usually without changing the exterior at all. In the particular turn-of-the-century block that we selected to study as typical of the neighborhood, the buildings were originally designed as town houses for moderately wealthy families. Over time, some have been divided up into three flats, some have been remodeled into a two-storey owner's appartment with a rentable flat above, and others have been divided and then converted back to a single-family town house, starting the cycle all over again. This flexibility, along with the mixed-use 'zoning policy', has contributed to the social and economic stability of the neighborhood by encouraging a broad range of income types and a broad array of local services and employment opportunities.

Our study-block houses a total of about five hundred people – in residential accommodations that include fourteen row houses, four apartment houses, and about twenty apartments situated on the second and third floors above sixteen street-level business establishments along one side of the block. This project was inspired by Andrés Duany's discussion of a block in Georgetown which has many of the same characteristics as this Chicago neighborhood. Duany refers to 'the neighborhood' – both as an institution and the physical manifestation of that institution – as 'the fundamental habitat of man', and aptly describes the block within the neighborhood as 'the DNA of the city'. Our project is intended to build a quantifiable argument around what should be obvious. Thus, we expect to clarify our position with hard data for those who require it.

All of this brings up that other, and equally important, dimension to the notion of permanence: namely the human and social dimension, which is a factor with its own rewards. It is the stability of a place that permits people to identify with it, and indeed social stability and physical stability (the architecture of a place) go hand in hand. Buildings such as the renovated Bond Hall of Architecture, referred to at the beginning of this essay, or the Audubon Society's building in Manhattan, or the remodelable Chicago row houses, are clear examples of this. For instance, Bond Hall was originally built to commemorate the Diamond Jubilee of the founding of the University of Notre Dame, and since then, thousands of students have experienced the building in one way or another. It has become for them an integral part of their experience of their college education: the building is a part of their memory of a place with which they may continue to identify, because this same building, even though it has changed in the functions it now accommodates, maintains important connections with the past. An old building has been given another lease on life, but this was made possible only because, like the remodelable traditional row house, it was built of durable materials in the first place.

The practice of naming campus buildings for principal benefactors or laudable individuals important to the history of the institution attests to the intention that each building should commemorate moments in the history of the school: each building is a thing of art and utility, serving to connect a community through memory across time. The Italian architect Aldo Rossi refers to buildings that remain in place while all else around them changes, as 'permanences'.

The philosopher Hannah Arendt wrote eloquently of how the communities and families that comprise the citizenry of a town or city are constantly reminded of the history that binds them by the lingering presence of familiar edifices of brick and stone. She goes so far as to suggest that the presence of permanent buildings within the fabric of the city is important to the natural human longing for immortality. In reference to the traditional European city, Arendt wrote: 'Nowhere else does the sheer durability of the world of things appear in such purity and clarity, nowhere else therefore does this thing-world reveal itself so spectacularly as in the non-mortal home for mortal beings [– the city]. It is as though worldly stability had become transparent in the permanence of art, so that a premonition of immortality . . . has become tangibly present, to shine and to be seen, to sound and to be heard, to speak and to be read.'

Ancient churches and cathedrals stand out as the most poignant examples of this, each serving, in Arendt's phenomenological terms, as 'a premonition of immortality . . . achieved by human hands'.

The traditional way of building, especially prior to the Industrial Revolution, held that important buildings should be constructed of durable materials on the assumption that they would remain useful indefinitely. It was an approach that presumed buildings would be remodeled and expanded to accommodate changing circumstances of use and ownership as time went on, as opposed to complete demolition and replacement as has become the more recent practice. Our break with the much older tradition of permanence in architecture disregards the role of architecture as a means to stability through the reinforcement of an effective and sustaining sense of place. In addition, built-in obsolescence consumes incalculable amounts of energy and non-renewable resources in the production of building materials, and considerable energy is expended and waste products generated in the process of demolition and reconstruction. The World Watch Institute's writers I cited earlier are convinced that, as we come to recognize that valuable resources are being indiscriminately wasted, we will return to some form of the earlier practices of 'building-to-last', rather than continue to build for the moment on the spurious assumption that the future will take care of itself. Those of us whose lives revolve around a university campus are all too painfully aware that the campus remains one of the last holdouts for the idea that each important new building should stand indefinitely.

At the time of writing, the Bond Hall of Architecture has completed eighty years of life. As its rebirth is celebrated, so is its eightieth birthday. We know that nothing actually lasts for ever, but it is not unreasonable to assume that Bond Hall will serve in its present capacity for another eighty years into the future. What is important here is not the actual number of years, of course, but rather the attitude – or the ethos or the frame of mind – that assumes that 'forever' provides a realistic time-frame for things and places that we hold as important.

Norman Crowe is an architect and academic.

THE CIVIC ORDER
David Selbourne

THE FUNCTION AND DUTY OF THE POLITICAL PHILOSOPHER
[I] This work is not only about duty but written from a sense of it: duty to the self, duty to one's fellows. Among other things, I take up and enlarge arguments first adumbrated in Chapter Eleven ('Citizens and Strangers') of *The Spirit of the Age*, published in 1993.

'The giant metropolis', I wrote in the above title, 'in which violent impulse comes increasingly to dictate the responses of half-educated strangers towards each other, cannot be the model of civic society'; 'randomly surviving social instinct, mutual fear, bureaucratic rule and stoical public spirit' are not sufficient to 'compose the civic order'; and 'mere payment to the state of taxes-for-services is not a citizen relation'. In such conditions, I argued, 'one law of common estrangement comes gradually to link all individuals . . . Individual rights, even when termed "civic rights", are shared in a phantom social order by all individuals, but between whom no citizen bond has been established. This parody of civic society . . . now increasingly stands for society itself. Socialism's failure, moreover, has (for some) ratified the parody as the only possible model of the social order.'

But, I suggested, the failure of socialism, with its false collectivities and uprooting of civic tradition, had also helped to clear the way for an understanding of the need to 'redefine and . . . enforce civic obligation, so that a true citizenship might begin to be restored to myriads of strangers'.

This is the theme of the present work, concerned not with the invention but with the enhancement of ideas of obligation; with ideas which are not so much unknown or misunderstood as forgotten. In its many variants, obligation is, after all, a long-established moral and political notion, even if today it is in eclipse.

Moreover, in the circumstances in which we find ourselves, as I set them out in *The Spirit of the Age*, I take it to be a particular moral obligation of the political philosopher . . . to promote the principle of duty on behalf of his fellow citizens, and as a means to recompose the civic order. He may be encouraged to the task by the fact that, despite the scale of civic disaggregation amidst which he lives, the civic bond – a term which, with others, I shortly explain – resists being attenuated to the point of breakdown. How so? Not least because of the efforts to sustain it of an enlightened minority of citizens. It is this minority whose numbers must be strengthened. Their enlightenment derives from an ethically active perception of the civic order; 'the principle of duty' is its expression.

There is, of course, a sense in which all this is known and has often been repeated, however fitfully, in our culture. The notion of citizen 'rights and duties' is routinely referred to in texts of political ideas; 'rights and duties' are paired almost by reflex. It is equally routine to find that, lip-service to duty once paid, generally at the outset of discussion, it is rights which are the dominating subject of discourse. Duties, never or rarely particularized, are soon forgotten, or alluded to in token or passing fashion as if their content and implications were taken for granted. If there are as many varieties of civic dutilessness as of obligation, then such failure to fulfill intellectual obligation is one.

Today, at a time of increasing civic breakdown, there is no shortage of practical moral talks to which the intellect is summoned. Yet in so many sterile and insouciant scholastic worlds, from which help might be expected to come in the moral resuscitation and refashioning of the civic order, often only effete erudition is to be found. On one side, there is a vain and overweening search for a new 'grand theory', or metaphysic, by which to make good the Marxist failure; on another, empirical technical study of microcosms ever smaller; on another, 'idle, lazy contemplation' and ethical silence.

I have written this essay on duty as a citizen among citizens, or a Jewish citizen-stranger, and not as a voice of authority, 'academic' or any other; nor, least of all, vicariously in the shoes of political power, but believing (with the Stoics) that the most important concern of philosophy is with individual conduct which bears upon our fellows.

THE CIVIC ORDER IN PRINCIPLE
[II 67, p71] In the civic order, as in the community, the individual lives a life shared with others. But in the civic order, whether that order be of the nation or of the city, it is a life ordered to civic ends; that is, to the ends of the

individual as a citizen. The citizen, whose membership of the civic order is generally unchosen and involuntary, and continues without the necessity of his consent, is more than a mere member of a community, or voluntary association of human beings linked by kinship, habituation, shared custom, or common interest. This is so, notwithstanding that community is historically prior to civic order as well as the first precondition of the latter's existence, and that a 'sense of community' is generally a powerful constituent of civic consciousness, and provides a strong impulse to the maintenance of the civic bond.

For the citizen is the member of an organized polity or body politic, whether of nation or city, which, however plural in its composition, is possessed of institutional coherence under the rule of law and a common ethical direction, is self-governing in whole (as in a sovereign nation) or in part (as in a city), and whose members are vested by virtue of their membership with generally unchosen and involuntary, but determinate, duties and rights.

Such civic order, whether of nation or city, exists to furnish its members with a refuge against their common vulnerability to the forces of nature, to provide them with security from the risks they may pose to one another, to promote by its actions their physical, moral, cultural, and material well-being, to safeguard the exercise of their civic rights and to enhance their mutual ethical relations by a just enforcement of the principle of duty.

This ordered community of citizens, or civic order, is by definition and necessity not a mere conglomeration or aggregation of people, but a coherently governed social body whose individual members are conscious of the civic bond, and whose actions are ethically determined by it. Where they are not, it is the duty of the civic order to enforce such ethic in the interest of all.

Nor is such civic order, when that order is the order of the nation, synonymous or co-terminous with 'the state', which is no more than an instrument of such civic order, in whose citizen-members, as a collective body, sovereignty ultimately resides. It is the civic order – not 'the state' – which is also the true locus of the 'public domain' or *res publica*, of which the city is a microcosm. Moreover, it is the ethical duty of the civic order, and of its instrument the state, to defend and enhance the sovereignty of the civic order – sovereignty being, *inter alia*, a principle of cohesion in the civic order – in the interests of the well-being of its members as a whole.

[II 73, p79] . . . The civic order may not, and arguably cannot, arrange the affairs of its members 'to the best advantage of life and convenience'. But insofar as it constitutes, whether in the form of the nation or the city, a 'human refuge and place of cultivation', as Voltaire calls it, and is the inherited work of generations of endeavor, the citizen is, again *prima facie*, under an ethical obligation to prevent its disaggregation or dissolution by all means in his power.

Nor . . . does it require us to adopt, in the manner of Rousseau, oppressive and mystical arguments as to the primacy of the civic order over the individuals who compose it, so that we may explain or justify such *prima facie* obligation; nor to hold, with the philosophers of the medieval Italian *comune*, that without the civic order 'man is nothing, less than a man'.

[II 76, p83] The civic order – the Greeks' πολις (*polis*), the Romans' *civitas*, Hobbes' 'commonwealth', Locke's 'civic society' – is also the civic κοσμος (*cosmos*): a word which, for the Greeks, signified both the 'world' and 'order'. Thus, μικροκοσμος (*microcosmos*) is both the world-in-miniature and order-in-miniature. But κοσμος (*cosmos*), in addition, had the extended meanings of 'ornament' and 'honor'.

The *civic order*, in which life is ordered to civic ends, ends of public safety and well-being, and secured by the principle of duty, is also a civic *world*. Remote from the mere casual aggregation of men, its right ordering by its citizens for their common good is an *ornament*, or art, worthy of honor; an order, and a world, which by definition coheres.

Like the family and the community, such civic order, or civic world, is the epitome of human association. But, unlike them, its coherence is the work of institutions as well as of custom and habit, of the rule of law and not merely of choice and desire, and of constitutional and other formal regulation of its rights and duties as being public, not private, matters; in Greek, a single world, πολιτεια (*politeia*), stood for the civic order, citizenship and the constitution.

The *civic order*, whether of nation or city, is no mere genus. To be real, it must be particular, a particular civic order, with a particular history and evolution, particular collective memory and tradition, and particular heritage of past civic effort – which heritage it is the task of its present citizens to protect, adapt, improve, and commit to the similar care of following generations of members of the same civic order.

Each civic order is the product of a process of accretion, of a process of becoming a distinctive social entity, or social body, with its own civic existence, its own citizens, its own rules, privileges, and customs, its own political life, its own public buildings, markets, charitable bodies, hospitals, educational institutions, and so on. Nearly every civic order also possesses a history of past struggles for its autonomy or unity, or in self-defense against a foe; sometimes, too, of the imposition of common duties upon the citizenry in times of danger or crisis, sometimes of conflicts among the citizens over their various rights, claims, and needs.

More particularly, each civic order, whether of nation or city, has (often less palpably) its own character, atmosphere or ethos, much of which is known to, and understood by, its own citizens only. It has its own 'moral being'; that is to say, its own institutions (and habits) of mutual assistance, peace keeping, public provision, education, and religious observance, or their deficiency and lack. It has its own aesthetic, also; that is to say, its own outward appearance – 'if you have not seen Athens, you are a blockhead', declared Lysippus (fl. 434 BC) – dimensions, styles, materials, colors, textures, and configurations of buildings and open spaces. It has its own geography or location, natural environment, flora and fauna, and climate; and its own political and juridical system, that is to say, its own institutions and practices of public discourse and information, representation of interest, law-making, adjudication of disputes, regulation of rights, and enforcement of duties.

These are the means, and the means only, of the civic order, means which take particular forms in each. The end to which such means are directed, if it is to be real, must be a particular end: the well-being of the citizens of a particular civic order. Such well-being must also take particular forms in particular places and circumstances, but in general, and in its broadest and most necessary aspect, it signifies the citizens' physical safety, dignity and self-regard, health, knowledge, and the material means to the enjoyment of life in conditions of peace.

[II 79, p87] The terms *civic order* and *citizenship* are, in the first instance, derived from, and refer to, not the nation but the city; just as the word 'Zion' is derived from, and refers to, not a nation or a people but a city, the city of Jerusalem. Such derivation points also to one of the main traditional concerns of political philosophy in the matter of the civic order: the 'problem of scale'.

That is, beyond a certain size of territory or population, so it is argued, there can be no 'real' civic order. 'If the number (sc. of citizens in the civic order) increases to one hundred thousand', Aristotle declares (*Ethics*, IX, 1170b), 'it is not any longer a community'; the round figure of 'one hundred thousand', albeit plucked from the air, signifies to Aristotle a total from which a coherent civic order cannot be composed.

'An excessively large number (of people) cannot take on any degree of order,' Aristotle likewise insists in his *Politics* (VII, iv, 1326a); 'we know of no state with a reputation for a well-run constitution that does not restrict its numbers.' Why? Because, in Aristotle's judgment, 'in order to give decisions on matters of justice and for the purpose of distributing offices on merit, it is necessary that the citizens should know each other and know what kind of people they are' (ibid, 1326b).

Indeed, the Greek civic order, or 'city-state', like the medieval Italian city-republic, was of the scale of the modern municipality in extent; the civic order in the scale of the modern nation did not exist. 'The city,' said Plato of his own ideal (*Republic*, IV, iii), 'can be allowed to go on growing so long as it preserves its unity: thus far and no further . . . Only so will the city continue to be one city, and not a mere conglomeration of people.'

If it is also true, as Rousseau argues (*Social Contract*, Book III, Chapter IV), that in a democracy 'each citizen must be in a position to know all of his neighbors', then the democratic maintenance of the civic bond (and thus of the civic order) cannot be secured under modern conditions; the megalith of the metropolis, in particular, must either be ruled by draconian measures or abandoned to disaggregation.

[II 80, p88] But it is not so. There is in principle in the civic order, as I define it, and in most of its possible political forms, a civic place and role for all its citizens, notwithstanding the 'problem of scale': . . . the abandonment of the civic order, whether of nation or city, to its own tendencies towards disaggregation would represent abandonment by the civic order itself of a fundamental obligation to its members, dictated by the principle of duty. It would also import the negation of the civic bond, without the preservation of which the civic order itself must gradually founder.

[II 82, p89] . . . the duties and rights with which the citizen is vested are required to be made in other ways as immediate, and as direct, as can be practically achieved. In the interests of the civic order as a whole, and in the effort to halt and reverse the process of civic disaggregation, the citizen's privileges, benefits, and rights – as well as his duties – must in principle be as closely attached to locality, and to their local exercise, as is possible, including for the purposes of serving as sanctions of the principle of duty . . .

Thus, to the rights of local suffrage attached to residence must be added other rights, privileges, and benefits specific to increasingly formal membership, or citizenship, of the local civic order. Likewise, to duties of (for example) local jury service or taxation, wider formal responsibilities for the well-being of the local civic order, enforceable under the principle of duty, must be added. Furthermore, the civic order, whether of nation or city, however large in scale, is always capable of regional, provincial, and zonal subdivision in such ways that the duties and rights of the individual citizen can be given practical local meaning, and be exercised to practical local effect. The duties owed by the civic order to its members – including the duty of the self-protection of the civic order – also dictate that such practical and ethical solutions to the 'problem of scale' be found.

[II 92, p96] . . . The citizen, as a social being, has much on which he relies, and therefore much which he has a duty to protect and defend, in the civic order to which he belongs, however imperfect such civic order may be. The value – moral, practical, material, cultural, emotional – of such belonging may have been lost from sight, or its recognition be willfully refused by the citizen, or even be discouraged in the corrupted liberal order. But its value, an inestimable value, remains.

In the political vocabulary of mankind in all times but these, the very language of distinction between the civic and the non-civic, the city-dweller and the country-man, and the citizen and the stranger denotes such value: the value of the civic bond and of the civic order, perceived both as ethical values-in-themselves, and as values of a practical, cultural, and material kind.

Thus, the Greek word for 'citizen', already discussed in another context, is πολιτης (*polites*), or member of the civic order. But the word for a 'private person', close enough to our 'individual', is ιδιωτης (*idiotes*); a word also meaning 'layman', an 'ill-informed, ordinary fellow', and, by further extension, 'idiot'. Its derivation is from ιδιος (*idios*), meaning 'personal', 'private', 'one's own', and, by extension, 'particular', 'separate', distinct', and by further extension 'peculiar' or 'strange'.

In fourteenth- and fifteenth-century Florence and Venice, for example, some two hundred to six hundred men at most were enfranchised in each city, and the power of officials was already such as to have begun to usurp the exercise of citizen rights. Yet it is plain from contemporary sources that the nature of the civic order, the values and virtues of citizenship, the distinction between *cittadino* (citizen) and *contadino* (country-man), and the dangers of civic disaggregation were widely and fully understood. The history of such civic knowledge – a history whose evolution has only recently been brought to an end in the corrupted liberal orders – is the history of the civic order itself.

At the heart of this history stands the etymology of the word 'civic'. Its root is in the Latin verb *ciere*, to summon.

The 'citizen' is he who is *summoned* by the principle of duty to assemble and take counsel with his fellows upon the safety and well-being of the ordered community to which he belongs. The 'city' is the place of such summons to duty; the 'civic' is that which pertains to, and flows from, such summons; 'citizenship' is the constellation of further duties, rights, and privileges which attach to the individual thus summoned.

The first or root meaning of πολιτης (*polites*), the Greek citizen, is not dissimilarly the defender of the citadel or πολις (*polis*), which by extension came to signify the city as a whole; the αγορα (*agora*), or place of assembly of the πολιτες (*polites*), is derived from the word αγειρειν (*ageirein*), to collect together.

In both Greek and Latin, the citizen, 'summoned' or with others 'collected together', is identified by his active co-responsibility for the security and well-being of the civic order, which is at the same time the source and guarantee of his privileges and rights: duty is citizenship's first term, right its second. Such citizen must, by definition, also possess the predisposition and capacity to exercise responsibility when called upon – as by giving counsel to the citizen-body, or otherwise protecting the civic order – for, without these virtues, such a concept of citizenship has neither substance nor effect; eligibility for office was regarded as a defining characteristic of Greek, Roman and Italian citizenship, and even as synonymous with it.

But in any civic order whatever, ancient or modern, citizenship requires the virtues which become a citizen, among them sufficient knowledge to act the citizen's part. When 'citizenship' itself signifies the possession of such virtue, to be a citizen is a proud boast; those who in his day falsely pretended to such citizenship, Epictetus tells us (*Discourses* II, xxiv, 2), could even be punished.

Moreover, from the root meaning of 'civic' derives that adjective of virtue, 'civil'. Thus, in Latin, *civilis* at first meant, neutrally, 'that which relates to a citizen'. It soon came, however, to signify 'befitting a citizen'; and, by further extension, 'affable', 'courteous', and 'popular'. The sixteenth- to eighteenth-century evolution of the English 'civil' followed a similar pattern. In 1494, it has the meaning 'pertaining to the community of citizens'; in 1526, 'befitting a citizen'; in 1606, 'polite'; in 1684, 'human'; in 1691, 'decent'; in 1716, 'educated' or 'refined'.

But in the twentieth century, and in the corrupted liberal order in particular, citizenship has lost such association with the extended meanings of 'civil'; to be a citizen and to be 'uncivil' are not contradictions in terms, for all that the ethic of neighborliness may, against the odds, survive. Nor could the specific notion of *civic virtue*, known to all times but these, prosper in conditions in which an individual may become a citizen by the mere issue to him of a passport.

Not only to Aristotle ought it to be preposterous that civic rights may be bestowed gratis, without ceremony or oath, and without correlative duty, *upon any individual whatever*; preposterous that any citizen whatever should take his place in the civic order, in conditions of accelerating civic disaggregation, *without civic education*; and preposterous that, in the corrupted liberal order, little ethical or practical distinction should be made between the rights, benefits, licences, and privileges of citizenship, but that all should be conflated as 'rights' under the rule of the politics of dutiless right, demand-satisfaction and self-realization through unimpeded freedom of action.

[II 92, p100] . . . consciousness of community, or of belonging to a particular community among the communities which compose the civic order, may in some circumstances make more difficult the vesting of the civic order with a common ethical direction. But it may equally serve as the means to a deeper understanding of the ethic of the civic bond, without the support of which no civic order can prosper. It is also as much the secret of the Jews' survival as it is of the survival of the civic order.

Civic sensibility, or civic consciousness, is also derived from and composed of *knowledge* of the civic order to which the individual belongs; of this knowledge, historic memory and familiarity-with-place are commonly parts. In particular, respect for place is both a source and an expression of civic sensibility, a respect which dictates protectiveness towards its appearance and aesthetic, as well as a desire for its maintenance, salvation from rapine, adaptation, and improvement.

In Pericles' funeral oration for the Athenians who had fallen in the first year of the Peloponnesian War (Thucydides, *History*, Book II, 38), he praises Athens for the beauty of its private buildings, a beauty to 'cheer the heart and delight the eye day by day'. Similarly, the citizens of thirteenth-century Siena declared it to be 'a matter of honor' that its officials should occupy 'beautiful and honorable buildings'. In Parma, the piazza was considered, under the city's ancient rules, a place of dignity deserving special protection; nor was 'respect for pure language and pronunciation', as Burckhardt tells us in *Civilization of the Renaissance in Italy* (pp241–43), the least of such cities' civic concerns. In the time of the Italian city-states (and in modern times too), pride in the city's appearance and individuality was (and is) an expression of civic sensibility, or civic spirit.

The possession of such consciousness implies more than a passive awareness of whatever beautiful and good things the civic order has inherited as a legacy from the past. It also dictates a custodial duty – if necessary, to be reinforced by sanction – to pass on such inheritance, unravaged, to the following generation.

[II 94, p103] . . . The a-civic, or those with no regard for the well-being of the civic order, 'we consider not as unconcerned', declared Pericles (Thucidides, *History*, Book II, 40), 'but as useless'. Αχρειοι (*achreioi*), with its sense of being unserviceable to others, is a word of truly civic judgment. Conversely, 'whoever conducts himself well', thought Kant (*Lectures on Ethics*, p7), 'is happy'; and to live as a citizen, or in civic fashion – *cittadinescamente viveasi*, Boccaccio called it (*Decameron*, Book II, 3) – was, until our times, seen as a means to such happiness.

Instead, the citizen, especially in the corrupted liberal orders, has been increasingly turned into a stranger not only to his fellows but to the civic order to which he belongs. With such estrangement, made profounder by neglect of the principle of duty as it applies to the citizen's duties to himself, his fellows, and to the civic order, the civic order itself must begin to fail.

THE PARTICULAR DUTIES OF THE CIVIC ORDER

[IV 289, p236] It is also a particular duty owed by the citizen to himself to show respect not only to his own elders but to the past of the civic order, where it is ethically worthy of such respect. 'Failure to respect the past', wrote Burckhardt (*Weltgeschichtliche Betrachtungen*, Bern, 1941, p50) 'is barbarism', provided only that such past is not barbarous itself. Associated with such duty is the duty owed by the citizen of respect for place, a duty which demands – and thus permits the civic order to expect and to enforce – the assumption by the individual of responsibilities of custodianship and care for the natural environment and material patrimony of the civic order to which he belongs.

Such duties of respect, in regard to persons, the past, and place (where they are worthy of it), are duties of self-regard also, since their fulfillment is a ground and source of the individual citizen's own self-esteem.

David Selbourne is a political philosopher.

Selected excerpts from the author's book *The Principle of Duty*, Sinclair-Stevenson (London), 1994; also Little, Brown (London), 1997, translation *Le Principe du Devoir*, Editions de l'Élat (Paris), 1997. Published by permission, copyright 1994 David Selbourne.

THE NATURE AND JUSTICE OF CITIES[1]
Carroll William Westfall

'. . . the Laws of Nature and of Nature's God entitle . . .'

In classicism, architecture is connected to and linked to and coupled with, fused with, united with, merged with, meshed with, and integrated with other products of people's actions. The shortest name for the largest realm within which all these actions of people occur is nature. The shortest name for the thing produced by the totality of these actions is the city.

The political life of the city is one form our understanding of nature takes; the architectonic structure of the city is another, although we must remember that the term 'architectonic structure of the city' refers not only to the aspects of one building but to the broadest sense of the tectonic form and formal character of the buildings, the equipment, the open places, all of them both public and private, comprising the urban setting of the city. This urban architecture, the essence of classical architecture, reveals what we aspire to achieve in our cities, and it assists or impedes us as we seek to fulfill our aspirations.

In the broadest sense, nature shows us how to live well, that is, with the best possible congruence with the highest qualities of justice in both our public and private acts. Art in the sense of artifice is the name we give to the technique of imitating nature. Architecture is the art of building in imitation of nature. Building well requires skillful use of a particular art just as do acting with compassion, grasping a truth, and fortifying the resolve to resist and battle an injustice.

Art, or more precisely, the proper art for each act, allows us to decipher and imitate nature. The imitation can be no better than the skill used to render it, but it can be wrongful, unwise, or incomplete if improper intentions pervert the products of even the most skillful artifice. Our aspiration for living in congruence with the highest justice must guide us to that which we ought to imitate in nature. But aspiration is not enough; we must also know how to apply our skill in imitating nature. And knowledge alone is not enough; it must be leavened with the wisdom necessary to understand facts as illustrations of truth. Wisdom is the product of maturity won through experience nurtured by private reflection and public discussion among people of good will, the product, in short, of the diligent exertions of the civil person.

Wisdom, truth, and the opportunity to practice reflection and discussion are hard-won possessions. To gain them requires a healthy skepticism about the possibility of having certain knowledge coupled with a sharp dialectical inquiry into the opinions of others, both those living and those long dead, about the important topics that the ongoing stream of unpredictable events presents to us, whether we want them or not. The world we live in is ever new, and therefore the questions we must confront are uniquely ours. Among the questions requiring a head-on assault as we work at building the just city today are these: How are we to live on a planet whose resources, we are learning at an increasing rate, are finite? How are we to live in a society that is increasingly riven by factionalism driven by fanaticism stemming from fervent beliefs, whether religious or political or agnostic or apolitical? How are we to improve our ability to live among one another in peace?

These new questions are as old as the classical city. They arise in that city, and addressing them requires attention to the experience that city makes possible, the kind of coordination of private and public actions available only in that city, and the support of private reflection and public discussion that only that city, the city devoted to justice, provides. That is, addressing them calls for the special skills of citizens imitating nature. Let us look at the questions in turn.

First, the limits of nature. In order to continue living on a planet whose resources are finite, the resources must be managed better by recycling, composting, and clever usage. In doing so, we will be imitating nature. However, managing our resources is one thing; using them for some purpose is another. To what end are we to use our resources?

The topic is taken up in the oldest surviving sustained discourse in philosophy, the dialogues of Plato which laid the philosophical foundations for the classical city. Early in the *Republic* (at 368–375) Plato explained that within the life of the city there is a difference between sustenance, abundance, and luxury. For any community, sustenance has one cost, abundance another, and luxury yet another, each step being more costly that the one before. As the costs increase, the character of the community changes. The important question is this: At what point does the character of the community change such that justice is no longer its principal interest?

In developing the argument Socrates establishes the idea that the city (or nation, or state, or polity – they are all the same word in this context) arises out of the needs of mankind and that the purpose of the city is to provide the means that allow its citizens to live in justice. Men need justice just as they need food, shelter, and clothing, but they often confuse the highest need, the need for justice, with desires for an abundance of what is needed for sustenance.

Socrates explains how a division of labor within the city supplies the necessities of life, including goods and services devoted to domestic exchange and foreign trade. Having established a secure supply for the necessities, Socrates asks the question we need to ask at the point we think our cities are complete:

> If [the city is complete], where are we to find justice and injustice in it? With the introduction of which of the elements we have examined do they originate?

The reply is important:

> I don't know, Socrates, unless they arise somewhere in the mutual relationship of these elements. (372a; Desmond Lee translation.)

'The mutual relationship of these elements'. A city is a whole collection, a body composed of related members, and the qualities of justice and injustice arise from the way they are assembled and used, not from the quality or character of any one of them.

Socrates continues by describing the life of the city devoted principally to justice. The citizens will have the food, clothing, and shelter they need, they 'will have wine to drink too, and pray to the gods with garlands on their heads, and enjoy each other's company. They will resist begetting offspring beyond their means lest they fall into poverty and war (this sentence, Paul Shorey translation) . . . So they will lead a peaceful and healthy life, and probably die at a ripe old age, bequeathing a similar way of life to their children' (372c-d). Life, then, is secure, marked by self-discipline, and devoted to what some now call the higher things of life.

Glaucon objects: 'Really, Socrates, that's just the fodder you would provide if you were founding a community of pigs!'

To Glaucon's desire for a more abundant life Socrates responds by compiling a list of what is lacking in the city devoted to justice but needed in a more luxurious society: couches and tables and other furniture, delicacies, scents, perfumes, call-girls and confectionery, the fine arts of painting and embroidery, and materials like gold and ivory. The population must be enlarged with hunters and fishermen; artists, sculptors, painters, and musicians; poets and their following of reciters, actors, chorus-trainers, and producers; manufacturers of domestic equipment of all sorts, especially those concerned with women's dress and make-up, wet-nurses, nannies, cosmeticians, barbers, butchers, and cooks; swineherds and cattle. 'With our new luxuries we shall need doctors too, far more than we did before.'

But there is more: 'If we are to have enough for pasture and plough, we shall have to cut a slice off our neighbors' territory. And if they too are no longer confining themselves to necessities and have embarked on the pursuit of unlimited material possessions, they will want a slice of ours too', and that will lead to the need for soldiers who will provide yet another range of people and goods the state must furnish.

The point is clear. To supply Glaucon's city of abundance will inevitably lead to war which might be against neighbors and will certainly be against nature. Glaucon asks: How much can we get for ourselves? Plato asks: What is the proportionate harmony between the city as something designed and manufactured and the natural world used as a source of supply? Can nature supply desires that are infinitely expandable? And where is justice in the balance? We have become accustomed to trying to satisfy Glaucon. Have we yet recognized that Socrates' city is the better one?

Socrates' city would be a spare place. If the ancient Romans had taken his lessons to heart we would not be impressed by their architectural and urban legacy. Building ancient Rome was costly, and in the early fifth century Saint Augustine called that cost into question. Grand as it was, Augustine said, Rome was a mere shell of a city because it did not seek justice first of all.

For the Platonist Augustine, what was true of the city was true also of the citizen. There is, he said, no justice in a city that does 'not give to the soul its proper command over the body, nor to reason its just authority over the vices' (*Civ. Dei* XIX, 24). This anthropomorphism also saw a city as a large house and a house as a small city. In both cases, the character of each must be immanent in the other. A mere collection of people does not make a family, a mere collection of families does not make a city, and neither does a mere collection of houses. People have to exert themselves to make families, families must work at making communities, and communities must devote themselves to city building. And then reciprocity can take effect: once the city has been made, the standards of justice it embodies can become embodied in its lesser units, namely communities, families, and individuals, and in the villages or towns and the neighborhoods and houses where they live. When that is done, each part, large and small, of the social and civil structure and of the architectural and urban structure will be the same but in different forms because each will be a form of justice. And they will all be imitations of nature since they will imitate the qualities of God who made nature and is knowable through nature.

Augustine asked much more of the city than Glaucon did. Although Glaucon's city takes many forms, each one appropriate for its end – the settlement, the market, the encampment, the pirate's nest, or any other banding together of people for some common purpose – it never puts the soul above the body or reason in command of the vices. Augustine's city has one end, namely justice or providing a means for each of its members to reach the full perfection of his nature, and it takes many forms, each one appropriate for current, contingent circumstances.

In the city of the Roman Augustine the private and the public life are mixed and mingled with one another. From that we can understand that purely private acts contribute nothing to our understanding of justice, just as purely private buildings, blocks, and streets produce nothing of public value. Privately built buildings, however, can produce public value when the building, the block, and the street are designed not as fragments deprived of a place within the larger public whole but as parts of a city, and are devoted to promoting public ends. The public life, after all, is a means of reaching ends that cannot be reached in private, and

this makes the public life something to treasure, even for private ends.

Standing at the head of the city are the buildings built by institutions for public purposes. For Augustine, they were churches, for Augustine the Christian understood that the Church was the earthly form of the city of God. Indeed, the best possible city man could build on this earth, the best city of man, was good to the extent that it served as host to the city of God. In the city of man justice was the earthly justice of an 'assemblage [of citizens] associated by a common acknowledgement of right and by a community of interests' (*Civ. Dei* XIX, 21). At its best, it produced an earthly peace 'in the well-ordered concord of civil obedience and rule . . . helpful to this life' (*Civ. Dei* XIX, 17), a peace that was valuable to the extent that it served the heavenly city which, 'while it sojourns on earth, calls citizens out of all nations' to participate 'in the perfectly ordered and harmonious enjoyment of God and of one another in God' (*Civ. Dei* XIX, 17). At its worst, when at peace and not riven by faction, it would become the kind of place Glaucon wanted, a place to enjoy for its own sake.

In the city of man, Augustine's antidote to Glaucon's city was Socrates' city Christianized as the Church and institutionalized with a Roman hegemonic structure governing the public affairs of cities and states. The Church gave new form to the earlier covenant God had made with the Hebrews and had renewed and fulfilled in the person of the resurrected Christ. To flourish, this covenant of justice needed peace, which was something that the states acting as the host of the Church seemed never capable of providing.

When the Founders of the United States set about establishing a new order for the ages, there appeared to be only one way to structure a society riven by factionalism driven by fanaticism stemming from fervent beliefs, whether religious or political or agnostic or apolitical: 'Congress shall make no law respecting an establishment of religion, or prohibiting the free exercise thereof; or abridging the freedom of speech, or of the press, or the right of the people peaceably to assemble, and to petition the Government for a redress of grievances'. Religion was disestablished, and open, free disputation that was to serve as its counterpart in investigating nature was protected. Now the question became: How is the covenant with justice to be translated into the public life animating the city?

The Founders provided a new form for the covenant

which they discovered through the imitation of nature when they based their regime on the natural-right doctrine of equality and freedom. The covenant concerning earthly justice that had formerly been vouchsafed to a hegemonic Church was now entrusted to the state. This new formulation lowered the level of justice the state sought to make available through its agency, but it did so for the good reason that with a lowered and partial aspiration it could provide a more secure basis for individuals to enjoy the fruits of liberty without causing the individual to lower his own aspirations for justice. To make those fruits of liberty available, the state had, as Augustine had put it, to produce an earthly peace 'in the well-ordered concord of civil obedience and rule . . . helpful to this life'. Anything more was up to the individual.

With the sights brought down off the mountain top and focused clearly on the plains where the city of man was built, it would seem that the abundant energies of a vigorous public life could bring peace to our relations with our fellow citizens. But something else has happened. In lowering our sights, we seem to have dulled our imagination of what the best possible city can be. In neglecting the likes of Plato or Augustine, we imagined our cities in Glaucon's terms, as the sources for economic prosperity and for personal security and the convenient purveyors of the goods Glaucon sought. We forgot that a rich city may be a mean-spirited place that concentrates its wealth in the hands of a few at the expense of economic justice for the many. We failed to see the police state within the secure city. And we overlooked the fact that as we built the convenient city for some, we were adding to the inconvenience, and worse, of others.

During this century, the use of land and the distribution of private and public investment has followed ever more rational and logical patterns and has become ever more the means of increasingly separating people of different classes, economic standing, and races, and inhibited the participation in the public life of the city. And the utopian vision became bankrupt: that all the people in the city could have dwellings supplying at least the minimum of light, air, and elbow room and forming parts of larger communities within identifiable neighbourhoods where fellow-feeling among diverse people could form. People who could make a difference in their public roles and private actions no longer imagined it was possible to help the citizens who needed help.

Our habits and laws now lead us to build a fearsome place. What we are building is law-abiding, but so too was the pagan Rome that devoured its enemies, its strangers, and its resources. But Augustine transformed that city into the city of man that could host the Church. It took a second Christian preacher and son of Africa to reveal to us in our secular city that being law-abiding is not enough. This is the way the Reverend Doctor Martin Luther King, Jr, put it when writing from the jail in Birmingham in 1963: 'A just law is a man-made code that squares with the moral law or the law of God. An unjust law is a mode that is out of harmony with the moral law . . . Any law that uplifts human personality is just. Any law that degrades human personality is unjust.' When the laws of the city do not comport with the highest form of justice and with the best aspirations of human nature, the city is unjust.

Plato's anthropomorphism and immanence and Augustine's recognition that the universal Church is hosted by a multitude of earthly cities lives in Dr King's declaration, 'Injustice anywhere threatens justice everywhere.' Our cities are built by our laws and our laws and our cities build us. Do they, like just laws, uplift us, or do they, like unjust laws, degrade us? We see the character of the citizen in the law. We use the laws to guide our actions in the physical world that sustains us. And we see the laws take physical form in the cities we build to facilitate the actions we wish to undertake in private and in public.

The question we must ask, the question that classical architecture requires us to ask and which can be answered architecturally only in the form of classicism, is this: Do our laws comport with justice? Since not everything is covered by the law, we must also ask, Do our actions comport with the justice we seek in our laws? Classicism furnishes us with ways to acquire the wisdom, the truth, and the opportunity to practice the reflection and discussion required to guide the actions acting as answers to these questions. It is, after all, the classical position within nature that allows our laws, our actions, and the architectonic structure of our cities to strengthen the covenant between ourselves and our maker.

Carroll William Westfall is an architectural historian and theorist.

Some of the material here was presented at the Congress for the New Urbanism II in Los Angeles in May 1994, and CNU III, San Francisco, in February 1995, and at the 'Stewardship of the City' symposium in Birmingham, Alabama, sponsored by Auburn University's Center for Architecture and Urbanism in February 1995.

THE CITY OF JUSTICE
Peter Murphy

The classical was born of the city. It is difficult to think of the classical inheritance in politics, aesthetics or in ethics without thinking of the city. The *polis* was, and has remained, both the embodiment and symbol of classical culture in its many and diverse manifestations. The difficulty for us today is that the twentieth century, and particularly the post-1945 era, has been a period of decline of the city; especially in North America, where the traditional city – the downtown or inner-city – sank into a morass of seediness, crime, and poverty. The city became a *noirish* symbol of fear, threat, and decline.

Both as cause and effect of this, more and more people in the course of our century fled cities for suburbs, and the consequences (aesthetically, psychologically, politically) were stark. In the early twentieth century – when suburbanization gathered pace – the motivation for the retreat from the city was largely romantic. The suburbs offered contact with Nature, in the form of private gardens for householders. This was not the sublime Nature of great mountain peaks or thunderstorms, but it was a Nature that was redemptive nonetheless. The city began, correspondingly, to acquire the reputation of seediness, vice, and corruption, and reality soon followed reputation; or else, the place vacated by the city-dweller was occupied by the corporation and government department and their functionalist offices.

The triumph of the ugly was accompanied by the withering of the city in our century. The power of beauty was born of the city. The Greek *polis*, the Roman *civitas*, the Italian Renaissance *comune* – all were crucibles for the creation of immortal beauty. The twentieth century was the century of the ugly. In Europe, where the politics of the sublime were responsible for atrocity after atrocity, the terrible became 'the normal'. The denizens of the New World happily were spared the descent into the totalitarian inferno. Like Kant before them, they watched the unfolding revolution of horrors from afar. By the mid century, the majority of them had retreated into their gardens. Where they maintained a political interest, they had become observers of events – fascinated, horrified, absorbed by the spectacle of the bestiarium of the Old World. In their gardens, twentieth-century suburban smallholders felt safe. When that safety was threatened, they would go to war to restore it. But these gardeners were not active citizens. They did not enjoy the public life. Their happiness was not a public happiness. They did not have the *energeia* of the ancient citizen. Their *faux*-smallholding (the suburban block) did not give them the independence of means to enter politics or the public life as an avocation. Nor did they look for such an avocation. Rather, they were 'national citizens' – onlookers who observed events, and in elections judged the behavior of the decision-makers who exercised power.

The things that suburbanites shared were not public things. They were not the public spaces of appearance where the *agon* of society was played out. The price paid for this was the triumph of the ugly. Not in the European (Old World) sense of the triumph of the will; rather, more simply, in the sense that beauty is the union of opposites – and without the clash of opposites, beauty has no incubator. Beauty only finds itself through the struggle of contending forces in the public arena. Beauty is the sense that no force can ultimately overwhelm another force. Beauty is the line that keeps the contending forces *apart* and it is the shape that keeps those forces *together*. The ugly lacks both shape and line. It is 'formless'. Nonetheless size, profusion, multiplication, and domination give the ugly a power. The denizens of the 'modern city' of suburbs learned to submit to the power of the ugly. They learned to expand, to multiply, to extend things, infinitely – without any sense of the city possessing a center or a limit. And without center or limit – without the things which bring forces together and simultaneously keep them apart – no beauty is possible.

This 'boundless world' promised its denizens much, but left them with less. In this 'worldless world', the majority of modern citizens now live. When modern citizens left the city proper for the suburbs, they did so for the promise of a romantic communion with Nature – the picturesque suburban garden, a smallholder's romanticism. They could fulfill through Nature (the suburban garden) the feelings of (pre-rational) safety or sanctuary that the communion with God once offered. At the same time, the suburban garden offered the promise of a kind of enchantment. What was lost in the twentieth-century migration to the suburbs was the continual education in reason; that is, the rational orientation of the actor, that comes through negotiating the public world. The public garden, footpath, café, and square had little (daily) significance anymore for the twentieth-century suburbanite. Yet these were the very spaces and places where the clash of opposing forces was to be seen and heard. From this public world, the suburbanite had retreated inward. Not just into the private garden, but the private garden of the *psyche*. So it came to be that in the twentieth century 'psychological' conceptions of art and politics dominated all others. What was lost was the development in citizens of cognitive emotions – the rational feelings required for a life spent in the public spaces of appearance. Wit, humor, love of talk, and so on were replaced by the melancholic search for security or by the 'appetite' for sensation, scandal, and shock.

What was further lost, as a result of this, was the productive power of connection. It is in the public places and spaces that one 'learns' to create the forms, the paradigms of art and existence; for it is in the public spaces of appearance, in the midst of the *agon*, that we are called upon constantly to make rational connections. The frequency of puns, wit, and humor in good public life is a playful preparation for connecting the unlike and the opposed. Creativity is neither the 'expression' of pre-rational feelings nor the 'protestation' of strong, sublime feelings. Creativity is the *highest form of reason* – the connecting of antipodes. Antipodal natures are rationally connected/joined by the forces of *line* (ensuring that no side is effaced) and *shape* (ensuring that all sides are joined together coherently). The forces of line and shape are essential aspects of the power of beauty. The beautiful thing has well defined parts and is a well shaped, proportioned whole. The power of beauty renders justice. That which is well defined and well shaped is 'fair' – 'fair' in appearance and 'fair' in substance. It has aspects of both aesthetical fairness and ethical fairness.

Fairness in this sense – justice as fairness – is not to be equated with distributive justice. This stands in contrast to the dominant theories of justice of the second half of the twentieth century which share a preoccupation, if not obsession, with the distributive aspect of justice. But distribution assumes things (in this case *common things*) to distribute. From where, and in what form, do those things come? Distribution presupposes a production, *poesis*, a poetics, of things. Such *poesis* in the late twentieth century is stalled.

The rational joy in creating/making has been marginalized. The feelings of pleasure in making and creating have been side-lined because it is only in the *res publica* that those feelings develop fully – for it is in the public world that feelings of rational connection are at a premium. In the public world, the various forces of society make their appearance. They are at odds; they clash. Citizens participate in the clash of opposites. But, at the same time, citizens are called upon to find a rational connection between antipodes – to find a pattern into which the oppositions fall, a pattern that allows them to cease the warring and establish an equilibrium. Such 'pattern making' is the basis of all creation/production. The making of the pattern (the mold) is the creative act that, in turn, makes production (the making of things) possible. To learn to 'make the pattern' is to learn the act of *kosmopoesis*. But where does one learn such a thing? Not in a school or a workshop, a household or a private garden – for there one learns to follow the pattern, not to *make* the pattern. One finds that in the *kosmopolis*, in the city that is universal, where citizens of many different talents, qualities, ambitions, and backgrounds have to discover, through antagonism and friendship, the *eidos*, the design of rational order that will not only accommodate their many-sided strivings but will immortalize them in a beautiful form.

'Fair' distribution is an aspect of defining and shaping this *eidos*. But only one aspect – perhaps not even the most important one. Distribution is always distribution according to a pattern, and the distribution of things that have been patterned. Distributive justice is thus dependent upon a sense of pattern making, and it is in the city that this sense can be developed most fully. The city has lines (boundaries, limits). The city center draws together things, people, events. The city is an education in *rational connection*. The epitome of this education is the collection of treasured buildings of the beautiful city. In them, line and shape are perfected. In them, the reason and justice of the city are brilliantly exemplified.

A society may exist with or without the city center and limit. But to spurn the city means, for the denizens of the late twentieth century, to deny themselves an education (a continuous education) in *kosmopoesis* – in the making of order out of opposition, in the patterning of a contestatory society. Without such an education, justice, happiness, and wealth for all of the citizens will remain out of reach.

Peter Murphy is a political scientist.

OF TWO FREEDOMS, THE POLITICAL AND THE ARTISTIC
Samir Younés

'. . . not the same is correct in politics as in poetry'[1] *Aristotle*

How does artistic freedom operate within a democracy? And what of its relation to political freedom? Some hold the view that the distinctions between political freedom and artistic freedom are so fine as to be impalpable. Yet, while the similarities may abound, one should be wary of assuming an equivalence between these two freedoms. We examine political freedom first.

The American Declaration of Independence considered freedom to be an essential, causal constituent of human nature, a natural principle.[2] Freedom was therefore not an effect which emerged from the circumstances of history, even though this freedom can only be experienced within the realm of historical circumstances.[3] Natural law, then, is a principle which precedes and engenders civil law and criminal law, which in turn guarantee freedom and the notion of duty that every individual recognizes toward others, within a larger concept of the good. This good, however, cannot be relegated to a matter of individual interest alone. For, as such, the good would be pursued solely with respect to parameters which are relative to the individual. In this case, when interests conflict, conflagration arises, because duty would be a matter based on the individual's self-interest alone. Freedom here, is concomitant with and proportional to that individual's power. Accordingly, the form of government that groups such individuals can be no more than an aggregation of private interests. Here, we are far removed from the concept of the common weal.

Contrariwise, the moral principle spoken of above suggests an authority of reason, within which individual duty and interest, and the larger idea of justice, come from a highly valued acceptance of the true and the good by a group of diverse individuals with different interests. This is so, because such a form of government guarantees equal freedom and justice to different individuals with divergent backgrounds and aspirations. The authority of reason, then, is the normative value which guarantees the cultivation of freedom while keeping power in check. This authority is given legitimacy by virtue of it being agreed upon by all who see in it the just protection of their individual as well as their collective freedoms. Thus, a law has authority because we

know why it is just and what is the form of this justice, and because we willingly accept its authority over our actions. Consequently, the concept of freedom as an agent of reason, perceiving the true and the good – in moral judgment for example – supposes a concept of duty. 'It is not the absence of motives that qualifies the individual's ethical freedom, but the character of these motives that marks free action', remarked Ernst Cassirer.[4] This duty derives from a general idea of the good, and is committed to realize this idea. Here, the attainment of justice is the aim of government, and the hope of its realization rests within the 'good life', of which the polis is a promise.[5] Reason and ethics are also the guides for power which cannot act as its own higher principle. Hence the necessity for law, to regulate power and uphold the true and the good by guaranteeing political freedom and, within it, artistic freedom. In such a perspective, political freedom is more encompassing than artistic freedom and is a precondition to artistic freedom.[6] Now, politics may encourage, discourage or prohibit various artistic traditions, and sometimes the very same artistic tradition finds itself identified with political régimes separated by diverse ideologies having little to do with the ideal state we described above.

Political freedom and artistic freedom share a common aspect with regard to the concept of external authority. In this sense, a principle is held to have normative value, on account of its universal applicability to a variety of individual contingencies which may or may not resemble each other. It gains its historical validity from having been the object of reflection of many minds from different provenances, and from the experience of centuries. Thus it is reason that principally validates the authority of a nation's laws, or an artistic principle. The withdrawal of the authority of reason will precipitate the collapse of that principle. Collapse will also occur if the authority of an artistic principle or an art form is imposed through the exercise of political authority. However, an artistic principle remains in the domain of artistic truth even if a political entity has abused its authority by prohibiting it or by applying it tyrannically.[7] In such situations, artistic freedom may be seen as a way of overcoming the constraints that might arise from political situations. Conversely, in a state where freedom thrives, the arts help to shape, satisfy, represent, and inspire spiritual and intellectual pursuits and lesser pleasures.

Art can also be used as one means – among many – for a sought-after freedom; and the French Revolution's call '*Aux armes! Aux arts!*' attests poignantly to this effect. Freedom can be a means to attain an end such as the 'good life' or the true. Freedom, however, becomes an end in itself only when it is threatened. But if the understanding of freedom is exclusively relegated to a *sensus individuationis* as opposed to a *sensus communis*, then the resulting political form is that aggregation of individual interests which we mentioned above. This can lead to the tyranny of the individual or of the group, or to what I have called elsewhere 'the tyranny of the private'.[8] Such a view transforms the constitutional guarantee that secures the citizen's inalienable natural rights, to confer a higher value to an individual's will – interpreted as 'right' – over the collective. This position has serious implications for the concept of freedom and its limits, because an individual, if not animated by a larger concept of the common weal, will necessarily interpret an affirmation of the public interest as an imposition. There is a marked difference between merely accepting another individual's freedom and rights, and understanding the individual's free will within the shared purpose of a larger common weal which is represented by a government or a city.[9] The danger is that the first case leads to the 'whatever someone wants to do' situation, simply because such a view of collective living seems to be defined by nothing other than the existence of a multitude of individual wills, never amounting to a larger view of the 'good life', beyond pragmatic matters of taxes, front yards, sewers, and clean streets.

From here arises the confusion between pluralism as the willful acceptance of various traditions, rules – political or artistic – and forms, which is a consequence of the tolerant humanism of a democracy, and an indiscriminate acceptance of *any* interpretation and opinion, which is done in the name of democracy but is ultimately a kind of random permissiveness. Is it surprising, then, that contemporary artists who apply this view to artistic freedom, produce work of a primarily private meaning – proudly calling it the self-referential sign – to the near exclusion of work and meaning destined for the public realm? Such a practice is of course protected in a democracy, even if some artists are bent on denying the *sensus communis* upon which a democracy is based. Therefore, the care that a democracy takes to protect self-expression extends even to those who give more prominence to their individual expressions and meanings, to their private *doxae*, while concomitantly excluding the larger symbols and meanings of their culture.

Here, a democratic society pays a high price when the *doxa,* as a tyranny of the private, turns against this very same society and assaults it on two fronts. It does so, first, by claiming that collective symbols and meaning no longer exist, and asserting that all we can really have are private *doxae*. This absurd extension of an extremely skeptical view of the world is characteristic of a bent of mind which is more disposed to reject than to affirm. This bent of mind would probably agree with Sartre's contention that 'hell is others', whereas 'hell' may very well be estrangement and isolation from others, as experienced by Descartes' solitary man observing the world. In addition, this mentality implies that no points of view can be taken, either out of fear of being interpreted as logocentric, or from an inane identification of the millennial search for collective meaning with tyrannical régimes of the right or the left. Conversely, anything that side-steps larger meanings is permissible, hence, the rabid proliferation of nominalisms. Here, the confusion between democratic tolerance and 'indiscriminate toleration'[10] contributes to the collapse of art as a symbolic mediation between the universal and the particular, the enduring and the contingent.

But the millennial traditions of art and architecture tell a different story of collective and individual meanings and freedoms thriving in their mutual confirmations and tensions. Much of what art depends on for external meaning can be seen in its relations to views about nature, to a truth, and to a reality. And much of what art depends on for internal meaning can be evidenced: for example, in its relations to a larger artistic tradition and the artist's intellectual freedom.

Artistic freedom here gains its value from the dialectical movement between these relations. Thus there are various genres of artistic freedom.

One genre is seen in the ways that art selects disparate beauties from nature and composes them to produce objects which claim to surpass her creations. Hence the notion of the ideal, seen for example in Zeuxis' painting of Helen, or Vasari's *natura vinta dall'arte*. Art, then, generalizes, in order to discover and reveal the essential. Painting, sculpture, and architecture all rely on anthropomorphism as a natural paradigm. Thus conventions based on nature are themselves natural. Art here freely imitates a selection of aspects of nature which are held as artistic truths, and relates the fiction of its own artifice to that truth. This free imitation is perhaps best expressed in the Aristotelian view that art imitates things as they ought to be.

Poetry states truth in a variety of allegories and helps access certain truths in ways different from the approaches of science. Far from being lies, poetic fictions allude freely to another order of truth: a verisimilitude which may or may not relate to a concrete experience. The more poetry departs from truth, the more perspectives and shades of meaning it provides. In this we sometimes delight in the great departure from a truth, and sometimes reject depicted actions which appear too improbable, even for poetry. For example, in *Le Cid*, Corneille, desiring to respect the Academy's rule that a play takes place in a fictive one-day period, assembled the most unlikely sequence of events. Rodrigue, the hero, who is engaged to Chimène, first avenges the honour of his father, who was insulted by Chimène's father, by defeating the latter in a duel. Afterwards, he leads an army to defend the city from the attacking Moors, whom he also defeats. Later still, he returns to the royal palace to receive honors from the king and reconciles with and marries Chimène. All in one day!

Horatio Greenhough's sculpture portraying Washington as a Caesar involves many fruitful fictions and parallels. The same can be said of Jean Auguste Dominique Ingres' *Apotheosis of Homer*, an extraordinary gathering featuring personifications of the *Iliad* and the *Odyssey*, as well as Pindar, Virgil, Dante, Longinus, Raphael, Racine, and Molière. By contrast, a depiction of a historical setting can rely on factual truth, as in Canaletto's views of Venice and London, or depart drastically from factual truth while still appearing 'real'. Consider, for example, Canaletto's *capriccio* in which three Palladian buildings: the Basilica at Vicenza, the Palazzo Chiericati, and a project for the Rialto bridge, are brought together in a characteristically Venetian composition. This depiction appeared so true that, according to

Francesco Algarotti, many Venetians asked about the location of that area of the city which they had not seen before.[11] John Soane's plan for the Bank of England, especially as painted by Joseph Gandy, alludes at once to a parallel to the Roman Forum and to a culture so admiringly conscious of the inevitable passage of time, that it prefigures the future state of its own architecture in ruins. Such *capricci* allude to another order of truth and a genre of artistic freedom. By contrast, other conceptions of art reject allegory altogether, as in the realism of the Dutch group portrait.

But what of the connection between the links and boundaries[12] which are proper to each art, and the artist's intellectual freedom? For instance, how is an architect to depict a naval victory in a monument dedicated to it? And more precisely, how free is an architect to commemorate such an event within the limits of architecture? Comparatively, how could a painter or sculptor approach the same subject? Both the painter and the sculptor can depict in a painting or a *bas-relief* the factual happenings, the number of ships, and the intensity of the combat. The painter and the sculptor can also use allegorical figures of war, pity, pain, magnanimity, or ruthlessness. Their arts allow for this kind of analogy. But this is not the case in architecture. The architect may have the rare luxury of choosing the location for the monument. The architect may also combine motifs which have historically been associated with victories and armies, such as a triumphal arch or perhaps a temple front. *Bas-reliefs* and even allusions to a ship's prow in some details may be used. Still, to achieve this commemoration, the architect can only attenuate the boundaries of architecture to a certain extent, beyond which the limits of architecture will be eroded. For instance, it would be totally indecorous to erect a building in the shape of a ship. For buildings are not ships, and unlike ships, they are static objects.

It was this clear understanding of the relationship between artistic freedom and the links and boundaries between the arts, between what an art can and should represent, that led A C Quatremère de Quincy – prophetically – to caution against falling into two errors. The first 'consists in *stepping beyond* his own art to seek, in the resources of another, an increase of imitative resemblance'.[13] The second 'consists in seeking the truth *short of the limits* of every art, by a system of servile copy, which deprives the imitation of the image of that fictious part which constitutes at once its essence and its character'.[14] In the final analysis, artistic freedom can be said to be indissociable from the links and boundaries suitable for each art. Thus, a universal application of the axiom *ut pictura poesis* should be taken *cum grano salis*; for what is available to poetry's modes of fiction is not to painting or landscape, and there is still less of it available to architecture.

Following this discussion one may ask: If the artist or architect's intellectual freedom is linked indissociably to the boundaries of their art, then what are the inward parameters influencing this freedom? First, as a thinker/maker, the artist or architect is free through reason and constrained by the causes and effects of the material world. For example, a pure aesthetic judgment is freer, in so far as it is less dependent on sensory perceptions. Moreover, the mind can be seen as having constructed and apprehended the phenomenal world in accordance with its own structures. Thus the confluence of the empirical experience of sensory perception, as well as the mind's own ordering systems, are then projected on to a part of the phenomenal world. Observe, for instance, how the *a priori* unity and befittingness with sensory material are inherent in the mind while it reflects upon itself and while it connects present experiences with earlier ones and with the material at hand.

Similarly, the architect's intellectual freedom is influenced by the way the mind associates present and past ideas, perceptions, models, and motifs in an *ars combinatoria* which includes collocation, composition, disposition, and distribution. These words, and others, infer that the architect reflects on three relationships at once. First, the building's internal order, the Vitruvian *ordinatio*, *dispositio*, and *distributio*.[15] Second, the aesthetic qualities of architecture, the Vitruvian *symmetria*, *eurythmia*, and *decor*. (*Decor* here is seen in the agreement between the building's character and its destined purpose.) Third, the building's *decor* in the sense of external relationship with a tradition or with the cultural context at large. *Decor* here addresses propriety according to custom, befittingness to the subject and utility of purpose. Propriety in the *aspectus* or appearance of a building is achieved through *probatio* or approval, and *auctoritas*, the authority of general acceptance. Thus the architect works at once with the material of a tradition as well as within it.

The scope of this freedom is evidenced in the distance between a type and a model, a tectonic allusion to a theory of origins, the faithfulness or departure from propriety, the selectiveness and mastery of the composition of elements, experience, introspection, self-criticism, and, of course, the architect's own genius.

Freedom is in the art's ends, and less so its means, which have to conform to these ends. Similarly, the attainment of justice is the aim of a government and not its means. All of this proves that the freedom to relate the fictive to the true and the real in the arts, while protected – or not – by politics, is evidence of another genre of freedom than the one allowed by politics. So, while there is a genre of freedom in the thematic, compositional, and allegorical methods of the arts in general, there is another order of freedom still, which is proper to the essence, ends, and means of each art. This propriety extends to national characteristics, social mores, climatic parameters, regional customs, and tastes as well as individual taste.

Samir Younés is an architect and academic.

Notes

1 Aristotle, *Poetica* 1460b 13n.

2 An opposite idea is the Kantian view that freedom is not an innate quality but rather a task that humanity poses for itself. This task is earned and maintained with difficulty.

3 See C W Westfall, 'Architecture as Ethics', in *Building Classical*, R Economakis (ed), Academy Editions (London), 1993.

4 See Ernst Cassirer, *The Myth of the State*, Yale University Press (New Haven and London), 1946, Chapter XVIII, pp287–88.

5 On the Aristotelian concept of the 'good life', see Westfall's 'Politics', in R Van-Pelt and C W Westfall, *Architectural Principles in the Age of Historicism* Yale University Press (New Haven and London), 1991, Chapter 2.

6 This is not to suggest that political freedom is the only condition for artistic freedom, for art is a phenomenon that is linked ontologically to the human character.

7 Conversely, the fact that we live in a period where individual will and freedom are regarded as more important than the collective will, does not for example invalidate the truth that the city's aim tends toward the betterment of all.

8 See S Younés, 'The Civic Art of the City Beautiful', in *Città Giardino, Cento anni di teorie, modelli, esperienze*, G Tagliaventi (ed), Gangemi (Rome), 1994.

9 C W Westfall, ibid.

10 'Indiscriminate toleration' is a phrase coined by Demetri Porphyrios in *Classicism is not a Style*, Academy Editions (London), 1982.

11 A Rossi discussed this 'analogous Venice' as a locus of pure architectural values. See his *L'Architecture de la ville*, L'Equerre (Paris), 1981, pp218–20.

12 A link connects at least two distinct entities, anchoring them to a place or a tradition, thereby assuring their identities without excluding the possibility of their separation. Through closure and containment in time and space, a boundary guarantees identity to at least two distinct entities without excluding the possibility of their informing each other; thus guaranteeing at once passage and distinction. Such a dialectic allows various fields or arts to inform each other without eroding the boundaries that assure for each its proper character, thereby maintaining intrinsic content (immanent meaning) and extrinsic significance (transcendent meaning).

13 A C Quatremère de Quincy, *Essai sur la nature, le but et les moyens de l'imitation dans les beaux-arts*, Paris, 1823. Introductions by L Krier and D Porphyrios, Archives d'Architecture Moderne (Brussels), 1980, p68; p81 English translation, J C Kent, italics mine.

14 Ibid, p86; p102 English translation, italics mine.

15 Vitruvius, *De Architectura*, II, 1, 2 and II, 2, 1.

THE CITY, THE ENGINEER, AND THE ARCHITECT
Alan Baxter

The essence and fabric of cities are formed largely by architects and engineers. These professions reflect the nature and interests of society and interpret its aspirations, but also contribute toward the formation of future societies. The technological changes currently taking place have inevitably affected the thought processes and the work of architects and engineers.

The traditional reasons for dense large-scale urban habitation have steadily been eroded, to the point that there now remains only one good reason for its existence; it is a very human reason, to which I shall soon come. Cities of pre-industrial times were created for defence and political control, for the exchange of goods and knowledge, and, finally, for social interaction. Cities of the Industrial Revolution were still descended directly from the older established urban pattern: workers needed to be within walking distance of their factories and goods were distributed in a three-mile radius by horse-drawn dray. The early twentieth-century city adopted the same pattern and added the commute by public transport from suburbs to center. The city thus grew again, but it was still essentially the same highly focused organism.

The city today retains some aspects of the early twentieth-century city, but it is effectively a different creature. Its capacity to be used as an instument of political control finally disappeared about forty years ago, as television and the means of mass communication displaced the public forum. Other changes have been largely due to our much increased mobility and our adaptation to spending time in transit. Manufacturing no longer depends on the proximity of a large workforce. The total number of workers has declined dramatically with increasing mechanisation as well as a shift to a service-based economy, and the factory or warehouse is now more likely to be found along a motorway junction than in the city. The workforce arrives by automobile, rather than on foot or bicycle, and manufactured goods are distributed by road rather than by rail. The paradox is that just as much of our industry has become friendlier in terms of noise and air pollution, we have zoned it away, increasing the time and energy spent by the workforce in traveling.

The same has happened with our now largely office-based work, much of which has been isolated and scattered around the outskirts of the city in the form of business parks – 'park' being a euphemistic term for the asphalted parking space rather than the romantic vision of a William Kent or Capability Brown landscape that it evokes. The exchange of most goods now takes place not in centrally placed markets serving the whole city or an urban quarter, but over a great, web-like network without a center. Cultural activity no longer revolves around the city center, theaters, and museums but is projected and assimilated by way of television broadcasts and videotape. Social gossip is no longer exchanged in the central square but is relayed by telephone and by e-mail.

Through our technology of rapid transportation, electronic communication, and mass manufacturing, we have replaced all but one reason for the traditional city. Yet this reason is the most vital one of all; it has to with our essentially gregarious nature. We need to live in close proximity to others, in a free yet ordered environment. If this right is denied, the essential cohesion of society breaks down, ushering in social instability and hostility between social classes, races, and generations.

Our intellectual and cultural richness depends very much on the random coming together of minds, even the accidental encounter on the street corner or in public transport. There is often great joy to be had from bumping into an acquaintance while walking down a city street, but quite the opposite in accidentally bumping into another car. Traditional cities allow random interaction between humans and we all admit to loving this freedom; we seek it out by booking our city-break weekends in Amsterdam and Prague, Edinburgh and London. I have yet to notice any adverts for city-break weekends in Milton Keynes, where accidental encounters have been designed out. The city is an essential part of culture and social cohesion, and we must ensure that it will continue in the future to foster pleasurable and stimulating concourse between people.

But this is easier said than done. How do we care for the city today? It is daunting to even attempt to understand the complexity of this great changing organism, but by being aware of its great value we are less likely to damage it through insensitivity. And this is where architects and engineers come into the picture. The increased appreciation for urban life has yet to affect our way of thinking as professionals. There is little leadership coming from the universities – I suspect academics are lagging several decades behind and have, in the meantime, become far too specialized. In both professional and academic circles, the behavioral patterns of humans seem to be more mysterious than those of giant pandas.

Human beings are not strictly logical, but we do know when places please and suit us. Unfortunately our education, strongly influenced by rational scientific thinking, prefers to ignore our more instinctive behavior. Engineers, even more than architects, tend to concentrate on objects that are quantifiable and more likely to yield to scientific analysis. Traffic engineers are a case in point, pursuing their fascination with perfecting abstract free-flow vehicular charts regardless of the broader interests of the population.

There are three issues I would like to address that affect the future of cities. The first is movement and transportation. The second is the sustainability of the environment – we now realize that the world is finite and indeed quite small. The third is our relationship to new technologies.

Movement is for many of us an essential part of our lives, our working and social routines. The ambition of planners and engineers to achieve maximal efficiency of vehicular movement is ill-conceived and ultimately unrealizable: it has eroded not only the city fabric but also the social cohesion of city-dwellers. The vitality of a society depends on direct interaction between its members, and in the past this has been easily accommodated within the traditional city. The city of the future must recognize the importance of the quality and freedom of movement of its citizens.

The automobile is a wonderful invention that can give great joy and a sense of freedom when used in appropriate ways and in good measure. By now, of course, this may sound somewhat contradictory. The parallel is perhaps wine – one of the best items of news in recent years was the medical profession's disclosure that a few glasses of wine per day are beneficial to an individual's health. The same can be said of the car: appropriate use can be liberating and pleasurable, excessive use leads to cirrhosis of the city and to addiction. We are no doubt still quite juvenile in our approach to private car ownership.

The self-centered political climate of the last decade has supported an over-reliance on the car and demeaned the value of public transport. Discussions on car-use have usually focused on cost accountancy, often through the projection of dubious figures, while the true cost to society of our over-dependence on the car is not discussed. Individuals who do not own a means of transport have found their freedom of movement severely curtailed over the last decade. Those who do own cars are increasingly frustrated that the promise of freedom is not so easily realized, and that efficiency of movement in cities is declining.

There is a general awareness of the impossibility of dealing with the projected growth of car-ownership over the next decade, but there are as yet no practicable proposals on how we might balance the desire for private transportation with the ability to provide for it. Self-interest governs most of the discussion around the immediate issues of traffic flow and parking space. For instance, a recent survey of a mainly residential area of London showed that the inhabitants' prime concern was to increase the amount of parking space while substantially reducing the flow of traffic; two things which are, naturally, difficult to reconcile.

Over-reliance on the car is the most obvious but not the only cause of human isolation. Certainly we need a degree of privacy in our daily lives, but excessive isolation can now be said to be something of a disease, encouraged by the breakdown of families and neighborliness, the advent of information technology, widespread zoned suburban housing, business parks, anonymous mega-shopping complexes, and video entertainment. It is no longer just the farm widow living alone who is isolated, but the population more generally. Passive non-interactive work, travel, domestic life, and private entertainment patterns cut people off from those social relationships on which their moral nature depends. This isolation can lead to despair and an explosive potential for intolerant and anti-social behavior.

Our ability to rub shoulders with our fellow humans while safely walking city streets and traveling on public transport is an essential safeguard of our tolerance of human diversity. We must enhance both the quality and the status of travel in company with others, not just because of the obvious major benefits of public transport, such as increased energy efficiency, but also because of the strong social cohesion and opportunities for random interaction that it generates.

How do we become mature in our attitude towards the use of cars? There are no easy answers but the starting point is an awareness of the broader issues. There are signs of better thinking in the British government planning policy PPG13 and in the recent Integrated Transport Strategy, which draws attention to minimizing the need for travel in major new developments. One or two Government Ministers have also raised their flags bravely in calling for quality in our built environment – to the horror of the Treasury mandarins with their over-zealous concentration on the financial side of things.

The second of the three issues I would like to discuss is the sustainability of cities. We now know that the availability of our resources – not just energy but materials – has limits, and that what we have already put to use is a resource we must not mindlessly throw away. The city is an investment we have inherited from preceding generations which we must respect, add our own investment to, and pass on to our successors. It provides for a better way of life and we have to accept it, warts and all. Some of the blemishes may be removed with gentle treatment, but the days of drastic surgery which nearly killed off cities like Birmingham and Glasgow are now over. These cities are at last beginning to recover, but others are still fighting for their lives.

The form and life of a city are only partly determined by the architecture of buildings. More important is the nature of the public realm, which in London over the last twenty years has been left at the mercy of numerous authorities with no supervising custodian and no greater shared vision for the future. Even a blinkered Treasury official can see that we have wasted a great deal of public money through lack of foresight about the consequences of our planning. But there are still many examples pointing to a lack of overall vision. New rail proposals had the potential to trigger significant positive changes to the nature of some urban quarters in London, but the issue was deliberately excluded from the rail developer's brief. We need, in short, to harness the energy from the often narrow and short-term interests of developers to a sensitivity toward longer-term horizons.

The fourth dimension – time – appears to be little understood by engineers. Members of this profession must come to appreciate that it is not easy to undo even the previous generation's interventions in cities. The new and impressive drive to revive the city of Birmingham is seriously hampered, not just by the enormous cost of removing the network of traffic flyovers, but by the constraints imposed by the unfortunate ring-road. Similarly, the vast multi-layered comprehensive developments of the 1960s are virtually impossible to remove without negatively affecting large areas in the vicinity. Once again, there are strong reasons for traditional streets with buildings sitting directly on their own foundations, the street simply responding to changes in the movement of services and people; this model would permit buildings to come and go as economic summers and winters occurred without affecting the entire urban entity.

Our knowledge of our total stock of buildings is astoundingly limited. Great numbers of redundant hospital and defence buildings are now being off-loaded to add to the surplus of industrial and commercial buildings. In Britain this coincides unfortunately with two other concerns: the need to rework existing nineteenth-century public buildings at a hundred-year interval, and post-war housing and educational buildings at a thirty-year interval.

For the first time ever, Britain has more than enough built floor-space. There is a reasonably stable population with a fairly static economy making a transition to greater awareness of the need for frugality in the use of energy and materials. The 1980s boom was driven by greed and often generated space of poor quality which we did not need. Of course we do need better housing designed in a manner more suited to our contemporary living patterns. But we never needed the mean minimum-cost, poor-value artefacts of the last few decades.

Meanness is a contagious disease that has been spread even further by the British government's insistence on cut-price fees, infecting some designers to the extent of reducing their quality of thought. The nation's new buildings and infrastructure now have a poorer long-term performance, making the related financial investment considerably worse. We must aim for better quality so that buildings and infrastructure are an asset and not a future liability.

Real conservation must come to play a greater part in the care of our cities. There is a thin dividing line between zealous preservationists who move to keep anything that has an age-value, often because of a fear of the new, and genuine conservationists who recognize the social and cultural value of re-using existing assets. Conservation is not about looking backwards. It is a creative act for today and tomorrow. It will become more important in our working lives as we move into a period of careful husbandry of all our resources: cultural, material, and human. To date, most of the focus in conservation has been concentrated excessively on individual buildings. Unfortunately, not enough people of influence care for the good husbandry of the city and the need to nurture its social vitality. Some interesting studies on the economic value of conservation have recently been carried out by several public bodies, including English Heritage. The Urban Design Group is also an important part of this discussion. Gradually we are coming to recognize that the vitality and attractiveness of a city depends not just on its architecture or the efficiency of its transport. We have difficulty in describing and measuring what makes some cities feel good to us, but we recognize this quality when it is present.

The third and last main issue I wish to address is the impact of new technology on the way we live in towns and cities. There have perhaps always been two strands in human thought, two distinct characters: the dreamer and the maker. Even as recently as 1850, in the first part of the Industrial Revolution, the two strands were closely allied. The rapid development of science generated greater specialization, which has spawned further divisions in the approach to making things. The dreamer's world has similarly split into many separate and uncommunicating strands. In our generation specialization is the norm; it narrows the ways in which we communicate and allows us to be dominated by technological processes.

We now have the promise of a new era where, instead of allowing machines to shape our thoughts and actions, we can use a much friendlier technology to fill the unnecessary and damaging gulfs between specialists and bring the two strands of dreamer and maker together again. We must stop being apathetic about the city. There is an all too great risk of continuing social disintegration, violence, and flight to segregated, secure suburban ghettos; as dying cities are left behind, the decline of culture and the privilege of citizenship follow soon after. We need not and must not follow that course. We have wonderful traditional towns and cities that we must respect. The engineer and the architect are the prime caretakers and we must use our new freedoms wisely.

Alan Baxter is a civil and traffic engineer.

This essay is a version of the inaugural RIBA/ICE lecture at the Royal Institute of British Architects, London, on 18 October 1994.

MODERNISM AND THE SEPARATED SELF
Louis Sass

A discussion of 'The Art of Building Cities' will naturally involve questions of an urbanistic, architectural, and political nature. Yet the new traditional architecture and urbanism emerge not from interest in the traditional city alone, but also from a critical view of much of what has determined the nature and quality of the built environment for the better part of this century. This essay by clinical psychologist Louis Sass helps to broaden the architectural debate from one of professional counterpositions to a more enlightened discussion that acknowledges some of the deeper motivating factors of modernist art and architecture.

Human action in our time, it has been said, lacks 'shape and measure' and is 'veined with currents of inertia'.[1] If so, this is surely related to a burgeoning of a certain introversion and alienation, the acceleration of an inner process that Kafka described in his diary as the 'wild tempo' of an 'introspection [that] will suffer no idea to sink tranquilly to rest but must pursue each one into consciousness, only itself to become an idea, in turn to be pursued by renewed introspection'.[2] It is in the modernist and post-modernist art and thought of the twentieth century that this self-generating, often compulsive process has reached its highest pitch, transforming the forms, purposes, and preoccupations of all the arts and inspiring works that can seem difficult to grasp, off-putting, and alien. This convoluted and paradoxical condition – so self-undermining and seemingly fragile, and yet so very persistent and adaptable – has endured for nearly a century without sign of exhaustion.

A BIZARRE TRADITION AND A TRADITION OF THE BIZARRE
The advent of modernism is the most distinctive and the most elusive of aesthetic revolutions. Virginia Woolf's famous statement, 'In or about December 1910 human nature changed', is not, of course, to be taken literally; but it does capture a widespread sense that profoundly new developments were occurring shortly after the turn of the century – developments concentrated in the realms of avant-garde art, literature, and thought, but echoing simultaneously in many other areas of human life. C S Lewis, a man of traditional tastes and tendencies, spoke for many when he wrote that no 'previous age produced work which was, in its own time, as shatteringly and bewilderingly new as that of the Cubists, the Dadaists, the Surrealists, and Picasso has been in ours'. Along with such critics as George Steiner and Roland Barthes, he saw the decades preceding World War I as marking the greatest rupture in the entire history of western art and culture; indeed, he considered modern poetry 'not only a greater novelty than any other "new poetry" but new in a new way, almost in a new dimension'.[3] The sheer fact of the newness may be indisputable, but defining its nature is a somewhat more difficult proposition.

All period concepts subsume a certain diversity, of course, yet the variousness of modernist innovations is somehow more daunting. What, after all, could dadaist art – celebrating chaos and mocking all aesthetic values – have in common with the ordered neoclassical formalism of the later T S Eliot? What could the austere rationalism of Mondrian or the Bauhaus share with the neo-romantic dream-logic of surrealism? Herbert Read saw the modernist revolution as unique in kind, precisely because it did not establish a new order; rather, he said, it is 'a break-up, a devolution, some would say a dissolution. Its character is catastrophic'. And another critic has written that if modernism were to establish a prevalent style of its own, it would thus deny itself, 'thereby ceasing to be modern'.[4]

It would be understandable, then, if one were tempted to abandon entirely the quest for an encompassing definition. Perhaps 'modernism' just has no unifying characteristics: Might the term designate an utterly diverse set of attitudes and practices, a mere miscellany sharing nothing more than a certain contemporaneity and, perhaps, a general aversion to the nineteenth-century traditions of romanticism and realism? In my view, such a conclusion is not warranted: though difficult, it is not impossible to discern certain family resemblances running through most central examples, not only of the advanced art of the first half of the twentieth century but also of the so-called post-modernist art, popular during the last few decades (I view post-modernism not as a deviation in some radically new direction but as an exaggeration of modernism's central tendencies (hyper-reflexivity and detachment) or as involving certain dialectical reversals occurring within a shared framework. To my mind, post-modernism is less an adversary than an offspring, or perhaps a sibling, of the high modernist period and sensibility).

Here I shall describe five key features of modernist art and its associated sensibility.[5] The first characteristic of modernism is the one most obviously associated with the heterogeneity just mentioned, and this is its negativism and anti-traditionalism: its defiance of authority and convention, its antagonism or indifference to the expectations of its audience, and, on occasion, its rage for chaos. Though precursors can certainly be found, notably in romanticism, it is in the twentieth century that these tendencies seem to have moved from an epidemic to an endemic state, thereby establishing avant-gardism, with its adversarial stance, as the 'chronic condition' or 'second nature' of modern art.[6]

The desire to escape conventional languages and seek as yet undiscovered subjects for expression is present in many classic examples of proto-, early, and high modernism. 'To inspect the invisible and hear the unheard of' – this was the goal the poet Arthur Rimbaud espoused in 1871;[7] and a great many writers and artists following him have adopted similar ambitions, as if only the ineffable and the incomprehensible could be worthy subjects for poetic attention. The twin motives this entails – escape from convention and exploration of the new – have often resulted in an extreme and off-putting degree of obscurity (the famous 'difficulty' of modern poetry) or even in a flirtation with silence, with total refusal of communication as well as expression on the grounds that any possible medium is inevitably contaminated by convention and the generic.[8]

A different attitude toward tradition and the possibility of originality has long been present in modernism, and has come to the fore under the banner of 'post-modernism'. Here, instead of being rejected, conventions are actually embraced and exaggerated in various forms of parody and pastiche.[9] The avant-gardist element, the alienation from tradition, emerges in a different way, not as an iconoclastic striving for radical innovation and originality but in the bemused and knowing irony, or deadpan detachment, with which conventional forms are mockingly displayed.[10]

The paradoxicality of entrenched avant-gardism is captured in the notion of an 'adversary culture' or 'tradition of the new', whose only constant is change itself, whose only rule is the injunction to 'make it new'.[11] By their very nature, such ambitions will incite the most varied forms of expression in an ever accelerating whirl of real or pseudo-innovation (or in the constant and ironic recycling of familiar forms). For the modern, as Octavio Paz has remarked, is 'condemned to pluralism'; characterized by novelty as well as otherness, it is truly 'a bizarre tradition and a tradition of the bizarre'.[12] We should not be surprised, therefore, that the common thread cannot be found in the forms themselves, but only in the psychological condition, the attitude of defiance or alienation, that underlies them.

A second, closely related, aspect of many modernist and post-modernist works is perspectivism combined with relativism, an uncertainty or multiplicity of point of view. We find works that draw attention to the presence of a particular perspective, thereby displaying a recognition of the inevitable limitedness of that perspective, as well as works that attempt to transcend such limits by inhabiting a variety of perspectives, simultaneously or in quick succession.

Both tendencies are inspired by the modern realization of the observer's role in both creating and curtailing the world of perception, a realization usually traced to Immanuel Kant's demonstration, at the turn of the nineteenth century, of the central role of the human subject, in particular of the human 'categories of understanding', in the constitution of all knowledge. At the limit, this amounts to what Nietzsche called 'the most extreme form of nihilism': the view that there is no true world, since everything is but 'a *perspectival appearance* whose origin lies in us'.[13] And this nihilism, this recognition of one's own centrality, can in turn be experienced in a couple of different ways: as a vertiginous sense of power inherent in seeing reality as but a figment of one's own, all-powerful self; or as a despairing recognition of the ultimate meaninglessness and absurdity of the human world, a succumbing to what Nietzsche termed 'the great blood-sucker, the spider skepticism'.[14]

The development in the twentieth century of what has seemed a higher sophistication about human consciousness has also been accompanied, oddly enough, by a certain fragmentation and passivization, by a loss of the self's sense of unity or capacity for effective or voluntary action; this, a third key feature of modernism, has gone along with an ethic of impersonality that contrasts sharply with the romantic cult of the self. One variant of the tendency might be termed an impersonal subjectivism or a subjectivity without a subject – a fragmentation from within that effaces reality and renders the self a mere occasion for the swarming of independent subjective events (eg, the fiction of Virginia Woolf or Nathalie Sarraute). A second variant indulges the most extreme objectivism. Here, life and the world are observed by a gaze that refuses all empathy and strips material reality of all the valences of human meaning (eg, some of the fiction of Wyndham Lewis and Alain Robbe-Grillet). Heidegger sees such extreme subjectivism and objectivism as existing in a kind of 'necessary interplay' or 'reciprocal conditioning' in the modern age: both being the product of a self-consciousness whereby the human being experiences himself as the essential being for whom and by whom the world is represented.[15]

A fourth, central characteristic of modernism is aesthetic self-referentiality. Many of the motives and purposes that animated earlier forms of art have lost their force in the twentieth century. Mimesis of external reality, evocation of a spiritual beyond, the conveying of an ethical or intellectual message, even the expression of intense inner feelings – all seem to have been deprived of their ability to compel commitment or belief. As if in compensation, many works of art turn inward, concentrating instead on the revelation of their own being, whether by focusing attention on their own material existence and internal structure or by displaying the processes of artistic creation and appreciation.[16]

In a famous essay, 'The Dehumanization of Art', the philosopher Ortega y Gasset treats many of the features of modernism I have mentioned, and in closing turns to a fifth feature of special importance – a particularly profound and pervasive form of irony and detachment. As Ortega sees it, one consequence of modern art's retreat upon itself is 'a ban on all pathos': given that depicting a realistic world of living beings is no longer a primary goal of modern art, such works can no longer engage compassionately with the sorrows and joys of normal human existence, but must operate instead in an 'abstruse universe' of 'purely aesthetic sentiments'. Rather than being imbued with a sense of sincere or passionate engagement, such art is therefore 'doomed to irony', to a spirit of waggery that may 'run the gamut from open clownery to a slight ironical twinkle, but . . . is always there'.[17]

This final aspect of modern art, which is even more prominent in post-modernism than in modernism, is implicit in most of the features already discussed, for they all involve disengagement – whether from the aesthetic tradition and the audience, from the perspective of the artwork or artist, or from experiential objects (be they external entities or reified subjective phenomena).[18]

PARALLELS WITH MODERN CULTURE

A number of related psychological tendencies that are more broadly present in modern society have been described by a small army of sociologists, anthropologists, philosophers, and culture critics of various stripes, writing over the course of the last century or more; and, surprisingly enough, there is considerable consensus on certain central points. It seems clear that one of the most distinctive and pervasive features of modernity is the intense focus on the self (both as a subject and as an object of experience) and on the value and power of the individual – emphases not to be found in the more communal, homogeneous, and organically integrated worlds of contemporary tribal and non-literate societies or in the culture of pre-modern Europe. The modern cultural constellation obviously has certain strengths – allowing as it does for freedom of movement and thought, and encouraging individual initiative and self-expression. But, of course, it also has a dark side; in particular, the forms of alienation summed up in the following list: 'isolation, loneliness, a sense of disengagement, a loss of natural vitality and of innocent pleasure in the givenness of the world, and a feeling of burden because reality has no meaning other than what a person chooses to impart to it'.[19]

The social historian Norbert Elias speaks of 'the extraordinary conviction carried in European societies since roughly the Renaissance by the self-perception of human beings in terms of their own isolation, the severance of their own "inside" from everything "outside"'.[20] This aspect of modern existence is manifest at many levels of cultural reality, not only in the realm of ideas but in characteristic forms of social organization, in cultural practices, and in the experiential modes of everyday life. For its most crystalline expression, however, we might look to the doctrines of the two most influential philosophers of the modern era, René Descartes and Immanuel Kant.

The essential implications of Cartesianism for the modern

self might be summed up in two words: disengagement and reflexivity. On this account a full realization of one's essential being – which is to say, of one's being as a consciousness – requires detachment from the body and from the passions rooted in it; for only in this way can one achieve the self-mastery inherent in recognizing and exercising the essential human capacity for rational self-control. The achievement of certainty in knowledge also requires disengagement – disengagement from naive acceptance of the existence of the external world in favor of an inspection, by the 'Inner Eye' of the Mind, of those 'clear and distinct' ideas that can only be found within (this is Descartes' famous method of doubt).[21]

Kant's philosophy, which was formulated at the end of the eighteenth century and is sometimes viewed as initiating modernist thought,[22] could be seen as a radicalization of Cartesianism, since it places an even more intense emphasis on reflexivity and disengagement. The *cogito*, the ego's awareness of the fact of its own consciousness, had played a critical role in Descartes' search for certitude; with Kant its role becomes even more crucial. Consciousness for Kant is not just a touchstone of certainty; now its structures – in the form of the (human) categories of time, space, causality, and materiality – are said to constitute, in a sense to create, the world of our experience. Acceptance of this suggestion had the effect (as Hegel put it) of 'withdraw[ing] cognition from an interest in its objects and absorption in the study of them, and . . . direct[ing] it back upon itself; and so turn[ing] it into a question of form'.[23] The Kantian vision also encourages a more radical sense of separation than did Cartesianism. In Descartes' scheme, the ideas we experience are certainly inner phenomena, yet nevertheless are assumed to be linked (albeit uncertainly) to an external world. Kant, by contrast, draws an absolute distinction between the realm of all possible human experience (the 'phenomenal' realm, as he called it) and that of actual existence or being (the 'noumenal'), thus implying an unbridgeable gap that sunders us eternally from the real – leaving us 'lonely and forsaken amidst the world, surrounded everywhere by spectres'.[24]

Nietzsche described his own age, and the two centuries to come, as the era of 'nihilism' – a word he used, in a complex and idiosyncratic way, to refer to various consequences, personal and cultural, of an exaggerated subjectivism. One central element of this nihilism was the disappearance of a sense of external grounding of values (something that occurs with the advent of Cartesianism and the Galilean scientific revolution); another was that devaluation of our experiential world that occurs when (as in Kant) it is contrasted with some hypothesized 'thing-in-itself' from which we are eternally separated.[25] In Nietzsche's view an important distinction had to be made between two types of nihilism: a passive kind that could be read as a sign of weakness, and more active forms that suggested vitality and will.

A similar analysis, also focused on subjectivism, is offered by Martin Heidegger. Whereas in the Middle Ages the world was understood to have been brought into being by a Creator-God, now it is 'conceived and grasped' as depending in some essential way on the human beings who know it. Here, then, according to Heidegger, is the 'essence of the modern age': 'the unconditional dominion of subjectivity' whereby the human being sets himself up as the ultimate subject before whom and for whom the world will appear as a kind of 'picture'.[26] The main problem with this glorification of the knowing subject (which, as mentioned, can result in both subjectivism and objectivism) is that it necessarily brings with it a devaluation of the world, whose ontological status is made to seem secondary, derivative, and somehow vulnerable.

Along with this separation from or devaluation of the external world has gone a polarization of the inner self from the outer or public persona, a polarization that has strong evaluative implications. Some time ago we began to live in a post-romantic climate that stresses not sincerity but authenticity – where the point is not so much to be true to other human beings as to be true to oneself, to fulfill one's own inherent being and potential. Similar developments are suggested by the gradual eclipse of the Renaissance category of *passion* – which implied some overt, often violent accompanying action – by the far more 'inner' or subjective concept of *emotion*;[27] it is also apparent in the growing prominence of notions of *dignity* at the expense of the older and more public concept of *honor*.[28]

One consequence of this inward turn has been a draining of value from public action, at least when the action accords with conventional expectation – for such action tends increasingly to be seen as irredeemably inauthentic, somehow compromised and contaminated by the demands of conformism and theatricality.[29] More and more, the true source of human significance, of what Wordsworth and Rousseau termed 'the sentiment of being', was felt to be located not in public action but in the idea of a private or unique self. There seem to be two or three main ways of responding to this set of cultural attitudes.

The first way of responding to the devaluation of the public self is to attempt to abdicate the public self entirely – either through hermit-like isolation or through refusal to interact in a more than perfunctory way – and this is accompanied by a tendency to locate the source of being in the hypersensitive tremors and yearnings of the inner life. Other, more active modes of being can also stem from the modern emphasis on individuality and the separation between inner and public selves. Instead of shrinking back from overt action, as from something inevitably contaminating, one may act in ways that display the sovereignty of the inner person or unique self. Usually, this will involve one of two characteristic attitudes (or both, for they are easily combined): a radical contrariness, in which one declares one's freedom from social constraint through the sheer *unconventionality* of one's behavior; or else a blatant inauthenticity, in which one flaunts the very *falseness* of one's behavior (which may itself be either conventional or unconventional) as a way of suggesting the existence of a hidden true self (or, at least, of emphasizing the illusory and superficial nature of the self that is visible). The last attitude, flaunted inauthenticity, is highly characteristic of post-modernism; it corresponds especially closely to Hegel's notion of the Spirit in self-estrangement, aware of the supposedly 'self-apprehending vanity of all reality', of the fact that 'everything is estranged from itself'. It follows that for the Spirit to 'be conscious of its own distraught and torn existence', as Hegel puts it, 'and to express itself accordingly – this is to pour scornful laughter on existence, on the confusion pervading the whole and on itself as well'.[30]

In *The Homeless Mind: Modernization and Consciousness*, the sociologists Peter Berger, Brigitte Berger, and Hansfried Kellner play out in some detail the effect that modern social, economic, and political developments have had at the level of individual experience. Among the consequences they see are the development of a certain anonymity and impersonality in social relationships, a heightened demand for rational planning and reflectiveness in everyday life, a rising sense of separation between one's social identity and a segregated sphere of individual consciousness, and the replacement of synthetic-intuitive by more abstract modes of thought and perception.[31]

Another contemporary sociologist, Anthony Giddens, stresses the unsettling quality of modernity's 'wholesale reflexivity' – which is turned not only on all traditions but even on the nature of reflection itself, resulting in the dissolving of anchored vantage points and a universal 'institutionalization of doubt'.[32] Certain theorists who see western societies as having moved into a stage of *post*-modernity emphasize a somewhat different set of developments, including a waning of deeply resonant emotion, loss of any sense of the real, and saturation by images and simulacra detached from all grounding beyond themselves.[33] It is not difficult to conceive the role such transformations might have – eg, by encouraging (or exacerbating) cognitive wavering and incertitude, predilection for ironic distance, and a sense of social withdrawnness or of dividedness or emptiness of the self.

It should be obvious that the various ways of disowning public action – whether via a withdrawal inward, unconventional behavior, or flaunted inauthenticity – do not spring from some domain entirely separate from the social order that is being fled or opposed. We can see this in the image of the creative personality that has come to dominate our age – a time when romantic individualism and expressivism have been transfigured into a far more radical aesthetic of isolation and detachment. Already in that 'bible of modernism in English', James Joyce's *Portrait of the Artist as a Young Man*, Stephen Daedalus describes the artist as remaining 'invisible, refined out of existence, indifferent, paring his fingernails'; and he embraces the artist's destiny as 'silence, exile, and cunning' – 'not only to be separate from others but to have not even one friend'.[34] Such a vision would have seemed most peculiar in the early nineteenth century, but by the beginning of the twentieth it had come to be a guiding cultural assumption in the west. It seems clear that this reflects widespread cultural changes, changes extending well beyond the domain of aesthetic attitudes. In this respect we might regard the artist as an emblematic as well as ambivalent figure – his inwardness, unconventionality, or irony providing an image of escape from or rebellion against modern society, while at the same time illustrating, in exaggerated form, tendencies that pervade this very same society.

Louis Sass is a clinical psychologist.

Selected excerpts from the author's book *Madness and Modernism*, BasicBooks, Harper Collins Publishers Inc, Harvard University Press edition, 1994. Published by permission, copyright 1992 BasicBooks.

Notes

1 H Rosenberg, *Act and the Actor: Making the Self*, University of Chicago Press (Chicago), 1970/1983, p9.

2 Kafka's diary, January 16, 1922, quoted in A Heidsieck, 'Kafka's Narrative Ontology', *Philosophy and Literature* 11, 1987, p250.

3 Quoted in M Bradbury and J McFarlane, 'The Name and Nature of Modernism', *Modernism: 1890–1930*, Penguin Books (Harmondsworth, UK), 1976, p20.

4 Irving Howe, 'The Idea of the Modern', in *The Idea of the Modern in Literature and the Arts*, Horizon Press (New York), 1967, p13. H Read quoted in Bradbury and McFarlane, 'The Name and Nature of Modernism', p20.

5 I offer an expanded discussion covering seven features of modernism in *Madness and Modernism*, BasicBooks, HarperCollins Publishers Inc, Harvard University Press edition, 1994.

6 See R Poggiolli, *The Theory of the Avant-Garde*, Harvard University Press (Cambridge and London), 1968, p230.

7 *Lettres du Voyant*, quoted in ibid, p215 ('inspecter l'invisible et entendre l'inoui').

8 See G Steiner, 'On Difficulty', in *On Difficulty and Other Essays*, Oxford University Press (New York), 1978, pp18–47; S Sontag, 'The Aesthetics of Silence', *Styles of Radical Will*, Dess (New York), 1969, pp3–34.

9 Leverkuhn, the hero of Thomas Mann's novel *Doctor Faustus*, asks, 'Why does almost everything seem to me like its own parody? Why must I think that almost all, no, all the methods and conventions of art today are good for parody only?' (*Doctor Faustus*, H T Lowe-Porter (trans), Vintage Books (New York), 1971, p134.

10 F Jameson characterizes this as a 'homeopathic expropriation' and co-option of cliché and of the machine; see *Fables of Aggression: Wyndham Lewis, the Modernist as Fascist*, University of California Press (Berkeley), 1979, pp70–82.

11 Phrases from Lionel Trilling, *Beyond Culture*, Viking (New York), 1965, pp xv–xviii; Harold Rosenberg, *Tradition of the New*, 2nd ed, McGraw-Hill (New York), 1965; and Ezra Pound.

12 Paz, *Children of the Mire: Modern Poetry from Romanticism to the Avant-Garde*, Harvard University Press (Cambridge and London), 1974, pp1–2.

13 F Nietzsche, *The Will to Power*, W Kaufmann and R J Hollingdale (trans), Vintage Books (New York), 1968, pp14–15.

14 F Nietzsche, *Beyond Good and Evil*, R J Hollingdale (trans), Penguin Books (Harmondsworth, UK), 1973, p120.

15 M Heidegger, 'The Age of the World Picture', in *The Question Concerning Technology and Other Essays*, W Lovitt (trans), Harper and Row (New York), 1977, p128.

16 Hegel had predicted that art would come to 'desire to find its satisfaction solely in its own in-dwelling as the true abode of truth' (quoted in E Heller, *The Artist's Journey into the Interior and Other Essays*, Harcourt Brace Jovanovich (San Diego and New York), 1976, p117.

17 J Ortega y Gasset, *The Dehumanization of Art and Other Essays*, Princeton University Press (Princeton, NJ), 1968, pp 21, 22, 46–47. As T S Eliot wrote, 'Poetry is not a turning loose of emotion, but an escape from emotion; it is not the expression of personality, but an escape from personality.' ('Tradition and the Individual Talent', *Selected Essays, 1917–1932*, Harcourt Brace, 1932, p10.)

18 On the disappearance of emotion and pathos in post-modernism, see F Jameson, 'Baudelaire as Modernist and Postmodernist: The Dissolution of the Referent and the Artificial Sublime', in C Hosek and P Parker (eds), *Lyric Poetry: Beyond New Criticism*, Cornell University Press (Ithaca, New York), 1986, p260.

19 Y F Tuan, *Segmented Worlds and Self: Group Life and Individual Consciousness*, University of Minnesota Press (Minneapolis), 1982, p139.

20 N Elias, *The History of Manners*, E Jephcott (trans), Pantheon Books (New York), 1978, pp250–51.

21 For discussion, see R Rorty, *Philosophy and the Mirror of Nature*, Princeton University Press (Princeton, NJ), 1979, p45ff.

22 See, for example, Clement Greenberg, 'Modernist Painting', in G Battcock (ed), *The New Art: A Critical Anthology*, Dutton (New York), 1966, pp100–10.

23 Quoted in C L Griswold, 'Plato's Metaphilosophy: Why Plato wrote Dialogues', in Griswold (ed), *Platonic Readings,* Routledge (New York), 1988, p150. It should be noted that I am primarily concerned with Kant as cultural figure, not with the details of his actual philosophical writings: the latter can be interpreted in a great variety of ways.

24 Friedrich Schelling, re Kant, is quoted in E D Hirsch, *Wordsworth and Schelling*, Yale University Press (New Haven, CT), 1960, p19.

25 See F Nietzsche, *Human, All Too Human*, H Zimmern and P V Kohn (trans), in *The Complete Works of Friedrich Nietzsche*, O Levy (ed), 18 vols, Macmillan (New York), 1909–1911; first published in 1878, sec. 16.

26 It is in this sense that man, in Heidegger's words, '"gets into the picture" in precedence over whatever is . . . set[ting] himself up as the setting in which whatever is must henceforth set itself forth, must present itself [*sich präsentieren*], ie, be picture' ('Age of the World Picture', pp131–32).

27 D M Lowe, *History of Bourgeois Perception*, University of Chicago Press (Chicago), 1982, p99.

28 Peter Berger, Brigitte Berger, and Hansfried Kellner, *The Homeless Mind: Modernization and Consciousness*, Vintage Books (New York), 1974, pp83–96.

29 This is part of what Richard Sennett means by the 'fall of public man'. *Fall of Public Man*, Vintage Books (New York), 1978.

30 Hegel, *Phenomenology of Mind*, J B Baillie (trans), Harper and Row (New York), 1967, p546, emphasis added.

31 Berger, Berger, and Kellner, op cit.

32 A Giddens, *The Consequences of Modernity*, Stanford University Press (Stanford, CA), 1990, pp4–6.

33 See Fredric Jameson, 'Postmodernism and Consumer Society', and Jean Baudrillard, 'The Ecstasy of Communication', both in Hal Foster (ed), *The Anti-Aesthetic: Essays on Postmodern Culture*, Bay Press (Port Townsend, WA), 1983, pp111–25, 126–34.

34 James Joyce, *A Portrait of the Artist as a Young Man*, Viking (New York), 1964 [first published 1916], pp215, 247. 'Bible of Modernism': Robert Langbaum, 'The Theory of the Avant-Garde: A Review', *Boundary* 2, 1, 1972, p240.

CONTEMPORARY PERSPECTIVES
Léon Krier

Today we can affirm fairly safely that the city of the future, or, more correctly, the cities of the future, will not conform to a single unified vision of whatever kind.

There exist universal principles by which to build good cities and villages. They transcend ages, climates, and culture. They are essentially anthropological principles, related to the habitual capacities of the human skeleton, body, and mind: streets and squares; cities, villages, and urban quarters; development programs and plots; building methods and architecture, of a certain type, size, character, aesthetic, density, and functional complexity are the unrenounceable axioms of urbanism. They are not to be confounded with the axioms of suburbanism.

The principles of traditional architecture and urbanism are not merely historical phenomena; they cannot therefore simply be declared outdated. They are practical responses to practical problems. They are as timeless as the principles of musical harmony, of language, of science, of gastronomy.

Modernism's philosophic fallacy lies in the infantile ambition to replace the fundamental principles of traditional architecture and urbanism in their entirety. Those architects who claim today to be inventing the architecture and urbanism of the twenty-first century are clearly even more foolish than the masters of early 'modernism'. Modernism can no longer proclaim itself, against worldwide evidence, to be the sole legitimate representative and embodiment of modernity.

Modernity and modernism are clearly distinct phenomena and can no longer be confused or amalgamated. Modernism is, like so many 'isms', born out of an excessive, possibly a pathological, desire for modernity. Like all forms of fundamentalism, it is reductive and tyrannical in its essence. If modernism wants to become a constructive part of the modern democratic world, it has to learn, at long last, that democracy is based on *tolerance* and true *plurality*; that indeed democratic tolerance, also in matters of architecture and urbanism, is based on a constitutionally founded reciprocity. Short of this change of attitude, modernism will become an item of outdated twentieth-century ideology.

Urban space is a void, a structured and structuring void; it has a hierarchy, it has dimensions and character, it cannot be just a left-over between haphazard building operations. Too much of it is a waste, a false luxury; too little of it, a false economy. All buildings have a public facade, acting positively or negatively on public space, enriching or impoverishing it. Streets, squares, and their numerous declinations are the optimum forms of collective space. Neither public nor private enterprise produces public space naturally as a mere by-product of its activities. Public space, the public realm in general, its beauty and harmony, its aesthetic quality and socializing power, never result from accident, but from a civilizing vision, and will.

It is not the age but the genetic capacities of the founding principles which ensure the quality of public space. Even one thousand years of suburban expansions will never parallel the civilizing power of urban foundations.

Urban centers are not called 'historic' because of their age, but because of the maturity and genetic power of their organizing principles. These principles are transcendent, and timeless. They are known to us; we can, if we so wish, build urban centers which will instantly have the qualities of so-called 'historic centers'. Also today, and on all continents, there are public and private buildings, sacred and profane buildings, buildings for families and buildings for large assemblies, buildings for rest and industry, for silence and for music, for isolation and gathering, for production and consumption, for hiding and for displaying. Architecture must be able to express contrasts, oppositions, characters, etc, in a non-ambiguous, evident, conventional, and accepted way. Architecture must be understood and accepted without explanation, or imposition of any kind.

The science and art of building cities, on the one hand, and the science and art of building suburbs, on the other, are fully known to us. Opting for the one or the other is not a matter of historical fate but of culture and political choice. There exist no valid excuses of any kind – neither social, nor economic, nor political, nor cultural, nor psychological, religious, historical, nor simply human – for building suburbs, for spoiling cities and land. Building cities is a responsible form of economic development; building suburbs is a corrupt form of economic development.

It is not history and age but structure and ideas which confer quality to an urban context. We are not interested in historic centers and architecture because of their age and history, but because of the genetic power of their organizing principles. The fact that a building by a great architect has existed for 500 years or for only one year, does not make a fundamental difference to its quality. It is its organizing structure and the sensuous quality of its materials and design which are decisive, not its age or historicity. The originality of a great building lies not in the age of its original material, but in the originality of its project.

In matters of Architecture and Urbanism, fundamental principles are of universal value, but realizations are always local and regional, adapted to specific climate, topography, materials, and industry; ie, to a geographic and cultural context. Only monumental architecture tends to transcend its regional origins. Although it is anchored to the vernacular of a region (Tuscan, Doric, Ionic, etc) or in the style of a dynasty or a sovereign, the artistic elaboration and symbolic codification of monumental architecture transcends place and origin and allows a near universal application; it represents a truly international style. Its power and validity are maintained only by strictly controlling its proliferation, by using it for exceptional and symbolically outstanding buildings.

Léon Krier is an architect and urbanist.

FROM THE ART OF BUILDING TO THE CITY
Introduction to the Projects
Norman Crowe and Michael Lykoudis

The return to traditional and classical paradigms for architecture and urbanism is shifting away from the reactionary movement aimed at countering the most damaging results of modernist thought and action, to the simple re-establishment of natural foundations. The role of regional expressions in architecture, the efficacy of evolved forms and practices, the logic and wisdom of long-held intrinsic urban values, and an active concern for nature and the sustainability of the built environment – these concerns, which we regard as fundamental characteristics of a civil society, can be found embodied in one way or another in traditional forms and practices.

The resurgent mainstream, as it were, is now increasingly regarded as the true center or heart of architecture and urbanism; so in theory we may say that, with the counter-revolutionary frame of mind in regression, the natural evolution of architecture and urbanism can return to the fore. Modernism, once regarded as a revolution that would change the way we would live in the future, has itself become a part of history, open to incorporation into the mainstream.

It is reasonable to expect that initial attempts to return to classical and traditional paradigms will tend toward rather stilted results, as the long-established rules are followed with inflexible precision. As experience is gained, this fear of erring usually subsides, allowing an inventive vitality to emerge. This is not to say that eventually the old 'rules' may be discarded, but rather that it is reasonable to assume that long-established guidelines and recognized principles may become sufficiently intrinsic to design that their application permits true invention while their active presence maintains the original *raison d'être*. Whether or not the present movement has fully arrived at this stage of comfort and self-confidence is, of course, open to argument. That being the case, the work included on the following pages may be taken as a test of how far we have come and the direction in which it all might be going. In this light, the work presented here – like the preceding essays –

serves as part of the dialogue also.

These, then, are some of the thoughts that account for the selection of the work which follows. We have included a broad range of projects and built works, chosen both from practicing professionals and from student work accomplished in the past few years at Notre Dame, in the expectation that the examples will speak for themselves. The intent is to illustrate something of the range of thought today that characterizes the return to traditional and classical paradigms in architecture and urbanism. At the same time, this selection demonstrates the rather close parallel being traversed by profession and academe. We do not attempt here to articulate the specific programmatic or theoretical guidelines for each project, but instead allow their aggregate presence to portray the intent.

We begin with the most basic of issues involved in the generation of architecture, the tectonics of construction – both its practical and poetic dimensions. This is followed by examples of private buildings, mostly houses, intended to be read here as mature manifestations of the primal task of architecture to house, shelter, and give order to the lives of individuals and societies. The next section is entitled Public Buildings, where it is hoped that expressions of the modern *polis* may be found in individual buildings dedicated to the public realm. This is followed by a series of Sacred Buildings, which may be considered a part, albeit a specialized subcategory, of Public Buildings. Next, we have grouped projects and works under the title of Public Places and Monuments. This section may be seen as a grouping parallel to Public Buildings, because although they are not themselves strictly buildings, their civic purpose and roles serve much the same objective. Finally, we feature work under two related headings, Quarters and Neighborhoods, and Cities, Towns, and Villages. Together, these represent the coming together of all that goes before, the ultimate intent of architecture: to comprise the true city.

INFORMATION BOOTH

Sandra Vitzthum

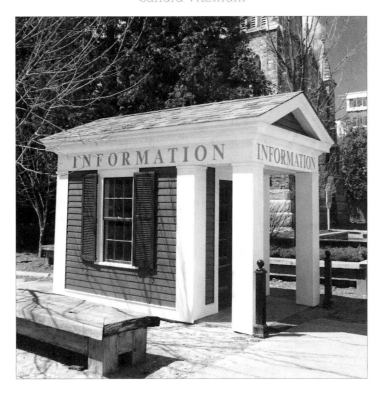

VILLA INDIANA

Duncan Stroik, Architect

THE ART OF PROPER BUILDING

Thomas Norman Rajkovich

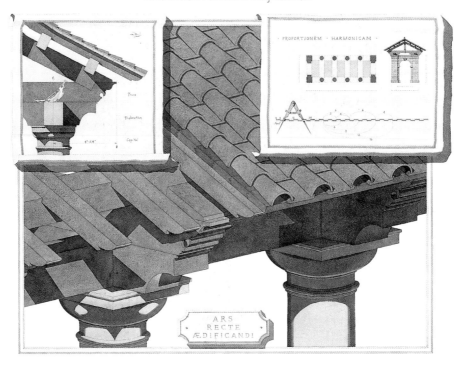

VISITORS' CENTER AND MUSEUM FOR MAYAN ARTIFACTS
La Maquina, Guatemala
Fifth Year Thesis. Student: Marie-Andree Soundy; Critic: Michael Lykoudis

DORIC AND IONIC ANALYTIQUE

Second Year Studio. Student: Anthony Bajuyo; Critic: Richard Economakis

THE WALLS, OPENINGS, AND ROOF FOR A DOVECOTE
Koroni, Greece
Richard Economakis, Architect

ARCHIVES BUILDING FOR THE UNIVERSITY OF NOTRE DAME

Fifth Year Thesis. Student: Sean Nohelty; Critic: Fr. Richard S. Bullene CSC

DORIC ORDER ANALYTIQUE

Second Year Studio. Student: Jennifer Rice; Critic: Duncan Stroik

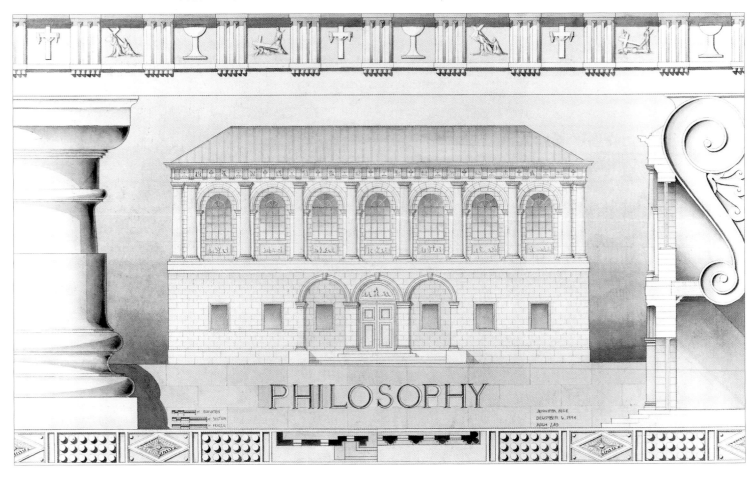

THE RELATIONSHIP BETWEEN THE NATURAL, THE RUSTIC, AND THE VERNACULAR

Fifth Year Studio. Student: Cristiana Gallo; Critic: Michael Lykoudis

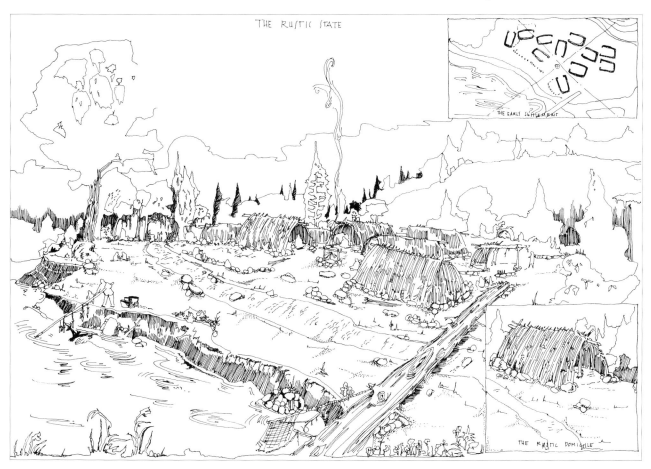

THE RUSTIC STATE

THE EARLY SETTLEMENT

THE RUSTIC DOMICILE

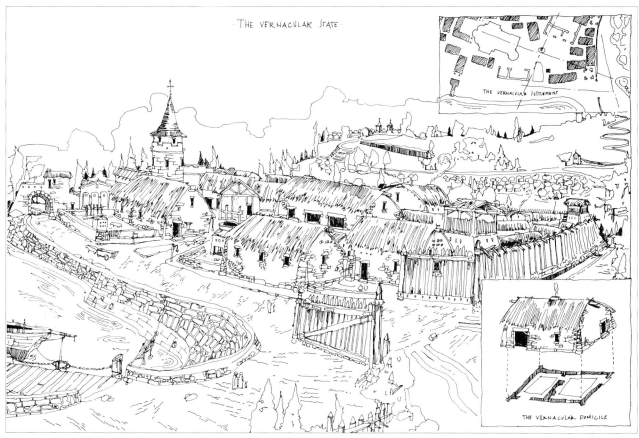

THE VERNACULAR STATE

THE VERNACULAR SETTLEMENT

THE VERNACULAR DOMICILE

Tectonics and Technical Issues

A PARALLEL OF BUILDING TYPES

Fourth Year Studio. Student: Jennifer Rice; Critic: Duncan Stroik

House Type   Palace Type   Shop Type   Religious Type

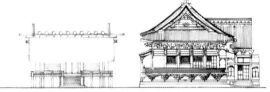

Japanese Typology

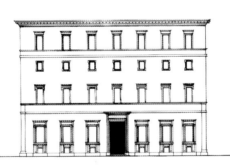

Roman Typology

American Typology

US CAPITOL CORNERSTONE
Washington, DC
Samir Younés, Architect

TECTONIC MODELS

Fourth Year Studio. Critics: Norman Crowe, Samir Younés, Richard Economakis, Cara Carroccia

Naigu Shrine, Ise

Norwegian Stave Church
Construction

Vernacular English Barn
Construction

English Hammer Beam
Construction

TOWNHOUSE
Houston, Texas
Curtis & Windham, Architects

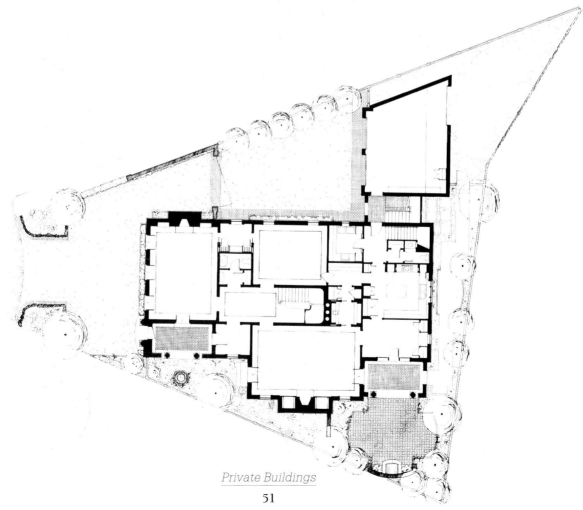

APARTMENT HOUSE
Chicago, Illinois
Fourth Year Studio. Student: Woong-Jae Park, Jeffrey Beam; Critic: Victor Deupi

Woong-Jae Park

Jeffrey Beam

APARTMENT HOUSE
Chicago, Illinois
Fourth Year Studio. Student: Atsushi Ishizaki, Karen Wolkerstorfer; Critic: Norman Crowe

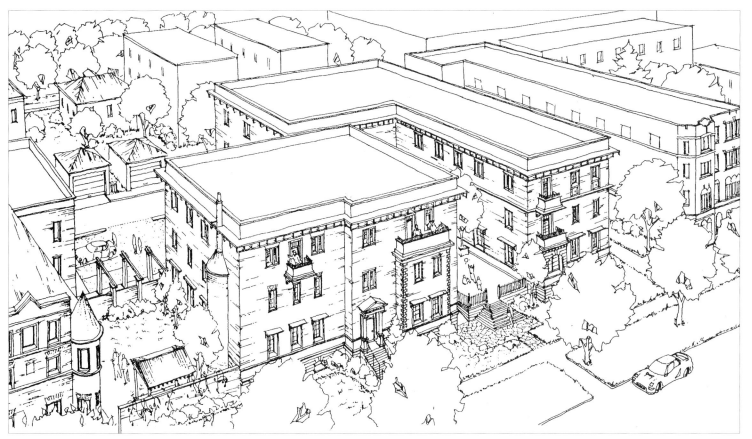

Atsushi Ishizaki

Karen Wolkerstorfer

Private Buildings

ZANITSCH RESIDENCE
Deep Creek, Maryland
Samir Younés, Douglas Devlin, and John Gissendanner

RESIDENCE
South Bend, Indiana
Michael Lykoudis, Architect

RIGGS NATIONAL BANK BRANCH OFFICES
Bethesda Office, Bethesda, Maryland; Northwest Office, Washington DC
John Blatteau, Architect

Bethesda Office

Northwest Office

Private Buildings

HABITAT FOR HUMANITY HOUSE AND STUDIO

Construction Coordinator: M Fitzgerald; Design Team: J Cruz, M Gago, S Tobin; Faculty Advisor: D Stroik

RESIDENCE ON RUE DE LAEKEN
Brussels, Belgium
Gabriele Tagliaventi and Associates

TOWNHOUSE
Chicago, Illinois
Fourth Year Studio. Student: Cristiana Gallo; Critic: Michael Lykoudis

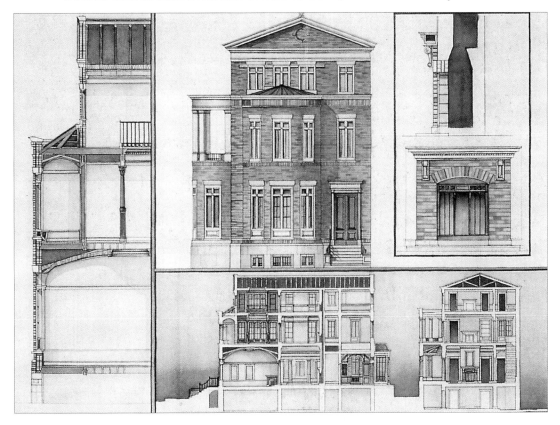

TOWNHOUSE
Chicago, Illinois
Fourth Year Studio. Student: Dana Gulling; Critic: Margaret Ketchem

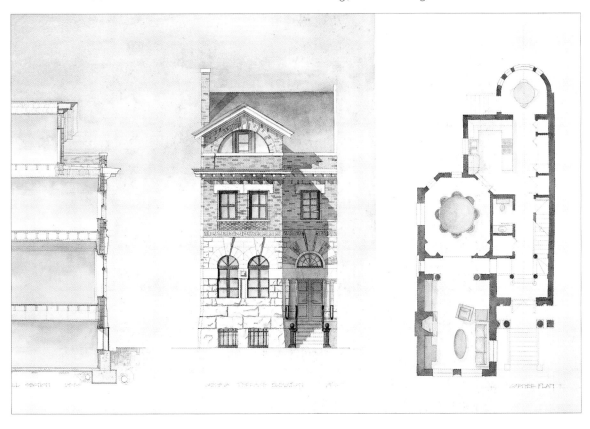

5 KONGENS GATE
Oslo, Norway
Piotr Choynowski

After

Before

Private Buildings

COMMERCIAL BUILDING
Birmingham, England
Porphyrios Associates

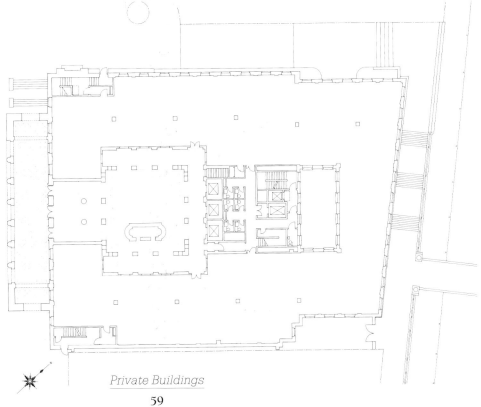

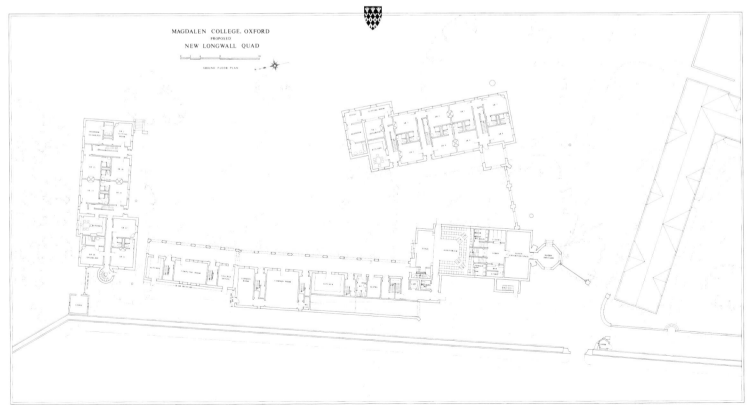

MAGDALEN COLLEGE, OXFORD
PROPOSED
NEW LONGWALL QUAD

GROUND FLOOR PLAN

Public Buildings

LONGWALL QUADRANGLE, MAGDALEN COLLEGE
Oxford, England
Porphyrios Associates

COURT AND GARDEN PROJECT FOR A PUBLIC BUILDING

Second Year Studio. Students: Tiffany Haile, Woong-Jae Park, Jaime Ortega; Critic: Richard Economakis

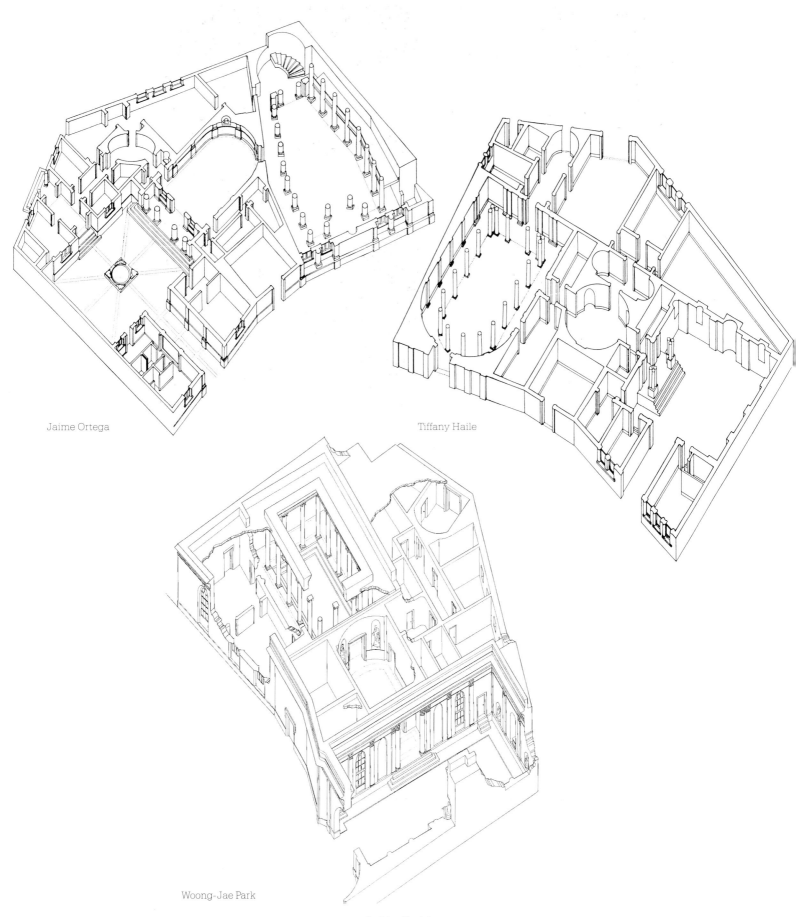

Jaime Ortega

Tiffany Haile

Woong-Jae Park

PUBLIC LIBRARY

Thomas M Felton, Architect

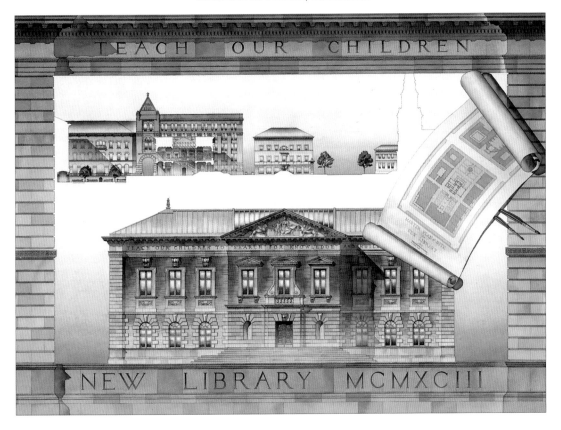

MUNICIPAL ARCHIVES BUILDING
Nappannee, Indiana
Second Year Studio. Student: Woong-Jae Park; Critic: Richard Economakis

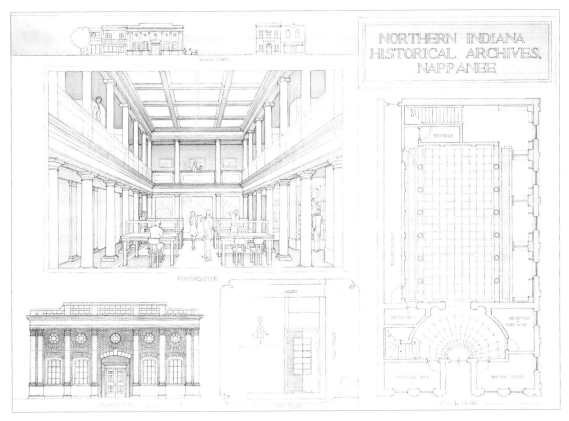

CULTURAL CENTER

Kyoto, Japan

Fourth Year Studio. Student: Laura Shea; Critic: Duncan Stroik

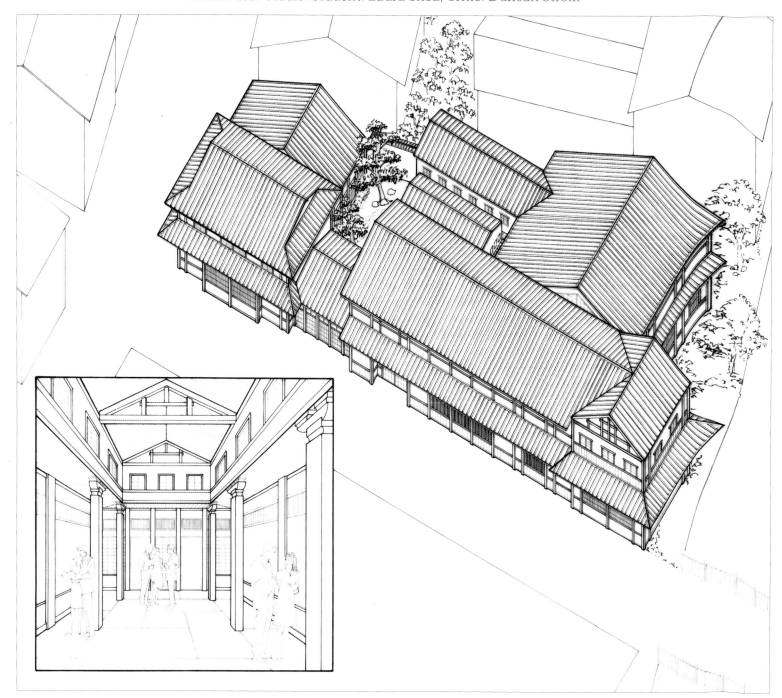

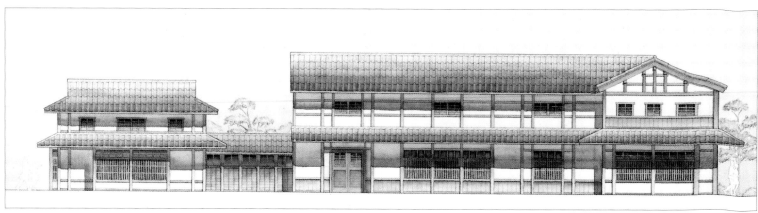

MEIGS FIELD AIRPORT TERMINAL
Chicago, Illinois
Fifth Year Studio. Student: M Damian Samora; Critic: Michael Lykoudis

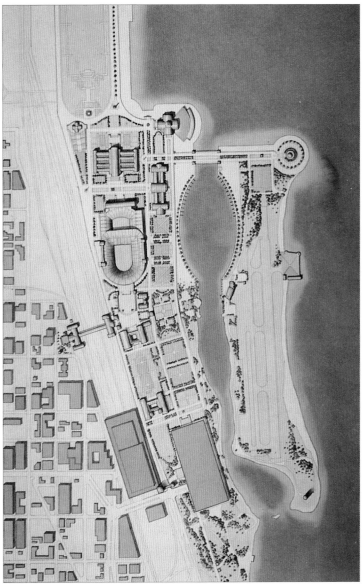

MEIGS FIELD AIRPORT TERMINAL
Chicago, Illinois
Fifth Year Studio. Student: Stella Papadopoulos, David Rodriguez; Critic: Michael Lykoudis

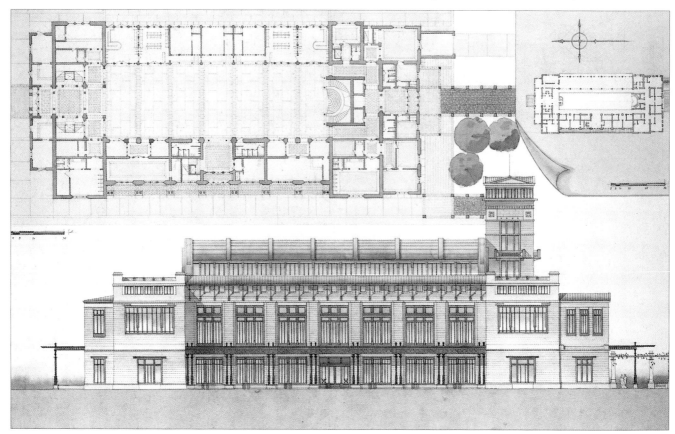

Stella Papadopoulos

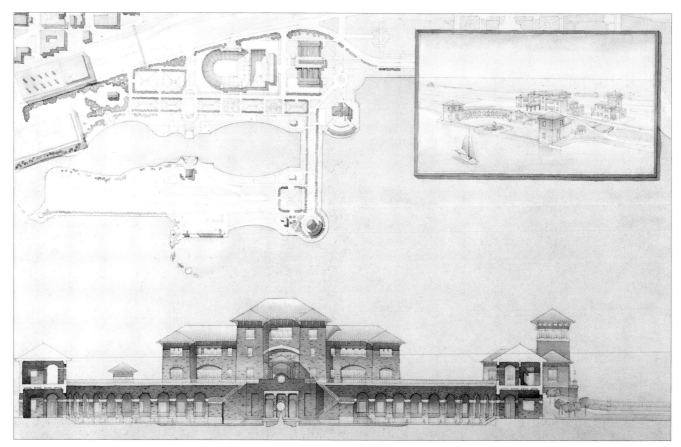

David Rodriguez

NEW SCHOOL
Harlem, New York
Graduate Thesis. Student: Stephanie Murrill; Critics: Richard Economakis, Michael Lykoudis

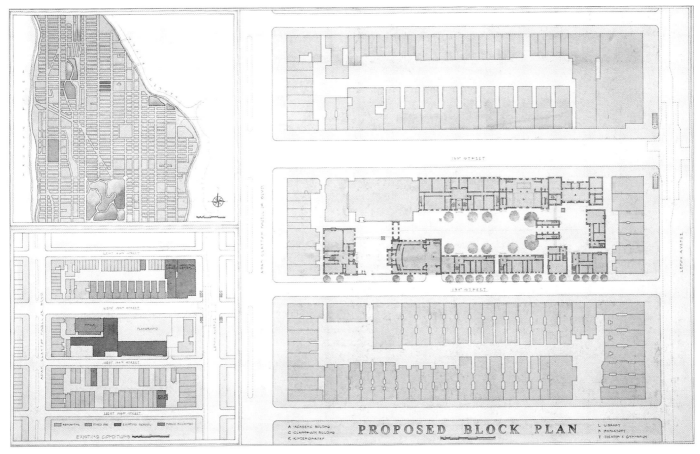

EXISTING CONDITIONS

PROPOSED BLOCK PLAN

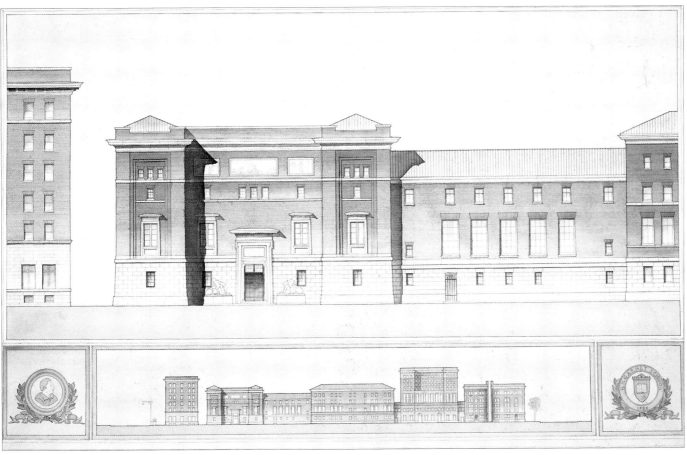

WINDSOR TOWN CENTER
Windsor, Florida
Merrill Hatch and Pastor, Architects

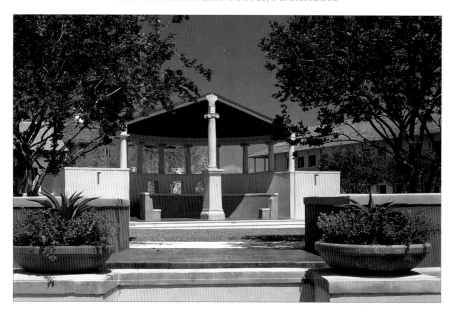

NATIONAL EQUESTRIAN CENTER

Washington, DC

Graduate Thesis. Student: Ashley Robbins; Critic: Michael Lykoudis

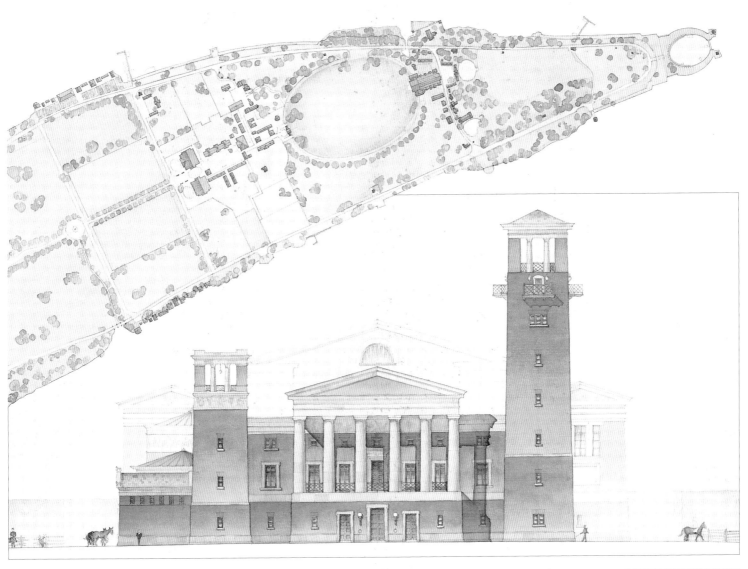

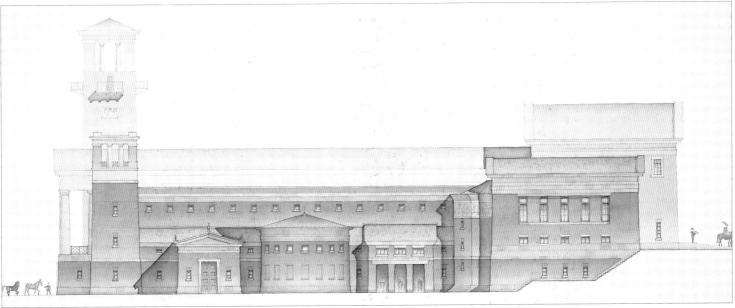

Public Buildings

CULTURAL CENTER

Kyoto, Japan

Fourth Year Studio. Student: Laura Shea; Critic: Duncan Stroik

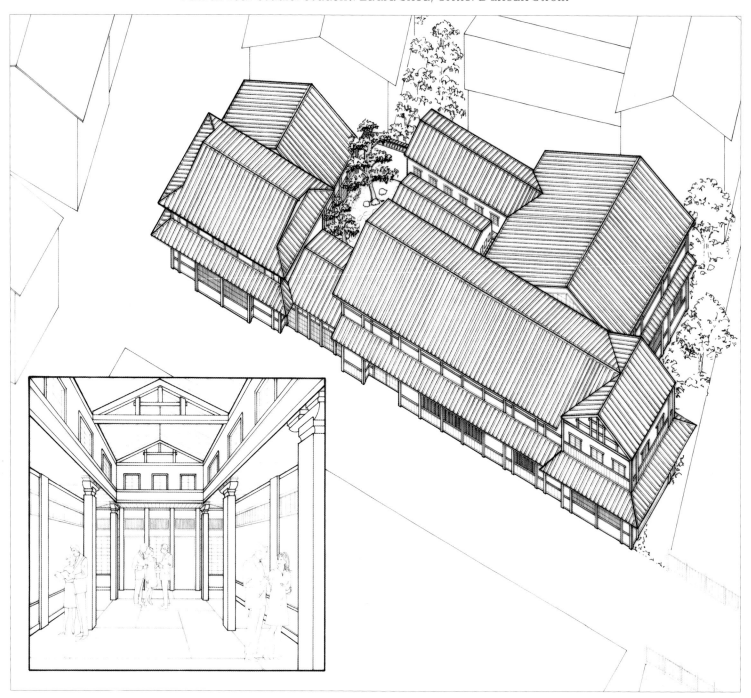

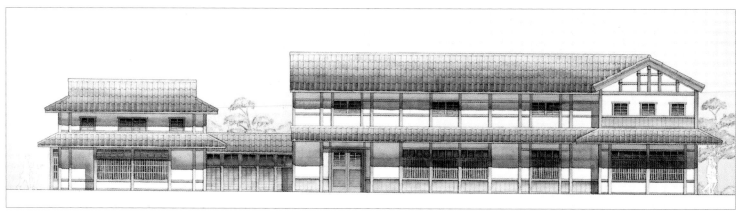

CULTURAL CENTER
Bukhara, Uzbekistan
Fourth Year Studio. Student: Ricardo Arosemena; Critic: Duncan Stroik

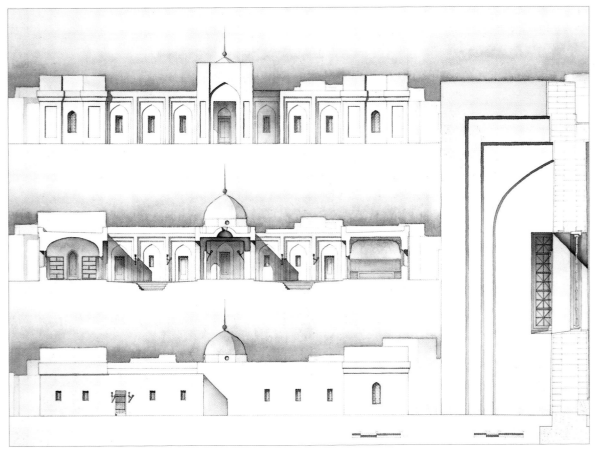

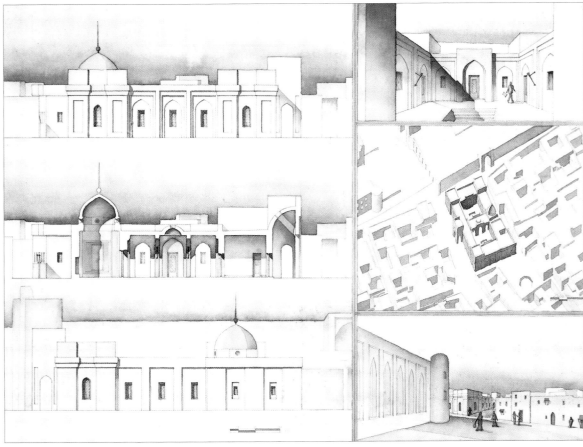

CULTURAL CENTER
Bukhara, Uzbekistan
Fourth Year Studio. Students: M Damian Samora, Laura Bossardt; Critic: Norman Crowe

M. Damian Samora

Laura Bossardt

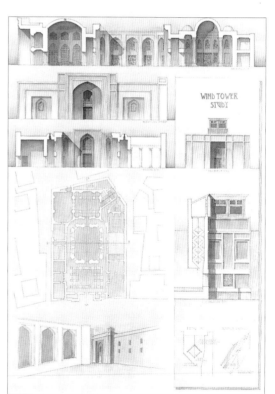

CULTURAL CENTER
Isfahan, Iran
Fourth Year Studio. Student: Geoffrey Locksmith; Critic: Samir Younés

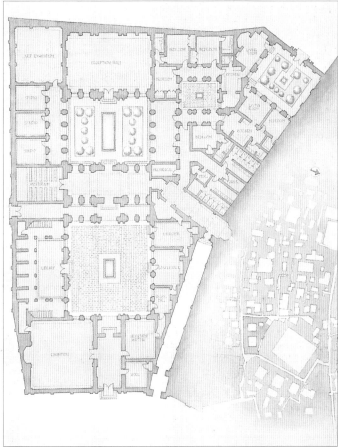

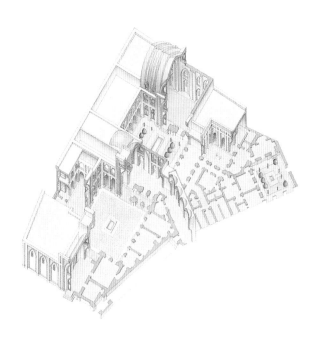

Public Buildings

STUDENT UNION AT DE PAUL UNIVERSITY
Chicago, Illinois
Graduate Studio. Student: Christine Finn; Critic: Samir Younés

MINOR LEAGUE BASEBALL STADIUM
Marshall, Michigan
Fourth Year Studio. Student: Malaika Kim; Critic: Richard Economakis

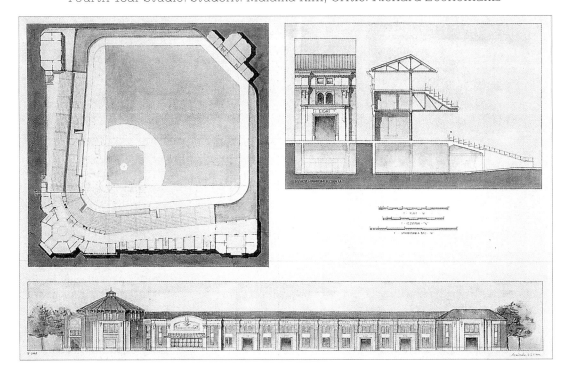

ARCHITECTURAL CENTER IN PARIS
Paris Prize Submission, Honorable Mention
Fifth Year Competition Studio. Student: Melissa DelVecchio; Critic: Michael Lykoudis

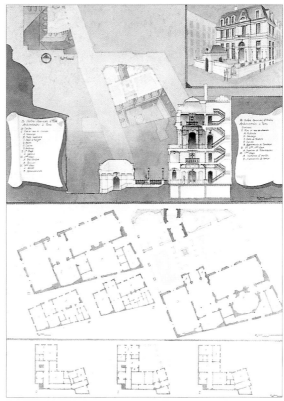

AULA IN ROME

Rome Graduate Studio. Student: Duncan McRoberts; Critic: Victor Deupi

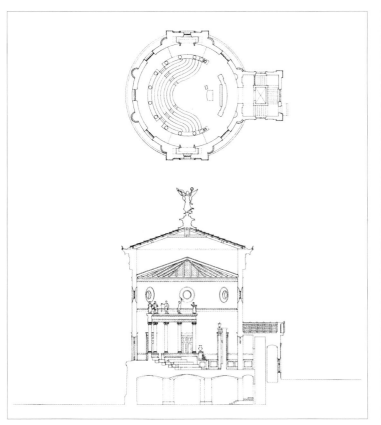

MARKET BUILDING AT PATERNOSTER SQUARE
London, England
John Simpson, Architect

THEATER AND SQUARE
South Bend, Indiana
Second Year Studio. Student: Woong-Jae Park; Critic: Richard Economakis

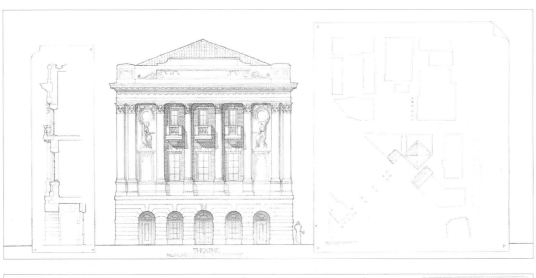

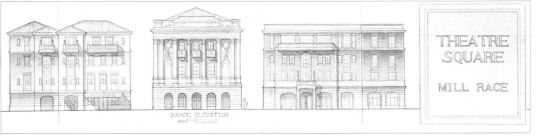

NATIONAL GENEALOGY CENTER

Ellis Island, New York
Fifth Year Thesis. Student: Mark Gage, Critic: Michael Lykoudis

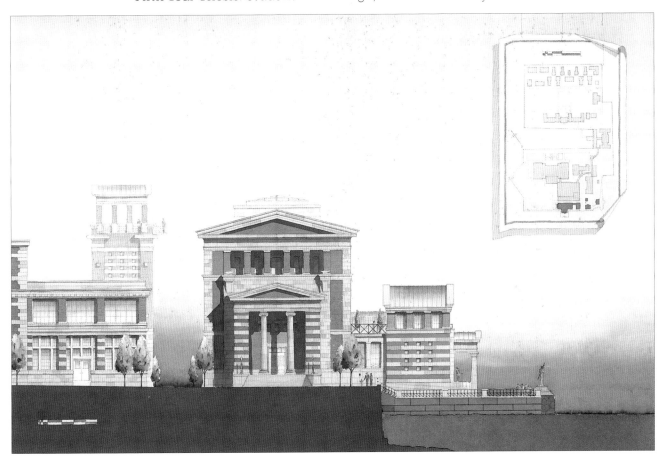

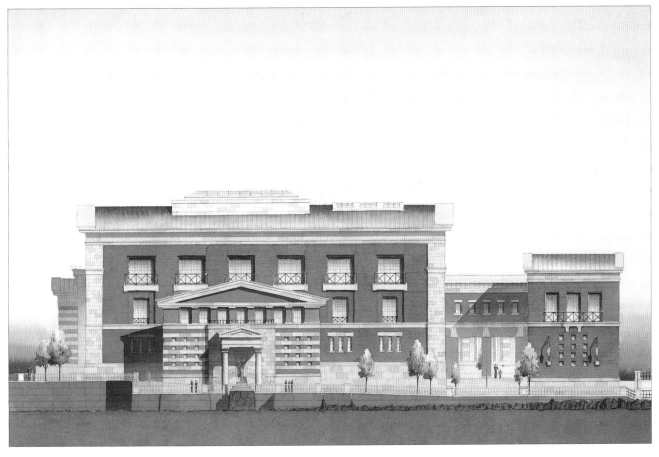

THE PINEAPPLE EXPRESS
A Railway Station for Stewart, Florida
Graduate Thesis. Student: Robert Pilla; Critic: Samir Younés

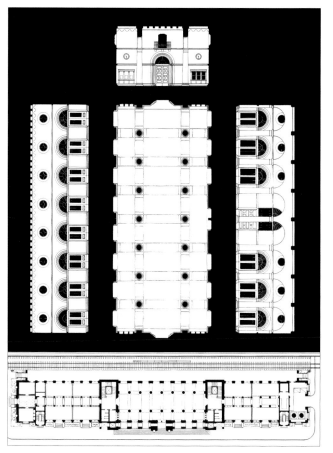

Public Buildings

A PARALLEL OF TWO SACRED PRECINCTS
The Stupa at Sanchi and the Agora at Athens
Fourth Year Studio. Students: Cristiana Gallo, Malaika Kim, Stella Papadopoulos; Critic: Michael Lykoudis

Agora: Spatial Diagrams

Stupa: Zoning Analysis

Agora: Site Section A-A

Agora: Spatial Analysis | Stupa: Spatial Analysis

Sacred Buildings

AMERICAN-CHINESE CHRISTIAN DISCIPLE CENTER
Chinatown, New York City
Graduate Thesis. Student: Rong Chang She; Critic: Thomas Gordon Smith

CATHOLIC CHURCH AND SCHOOL
Indianapolis, Indiana
Graduate Studio. Student: Braulio Casas; Critic: Samir Younés

MOSQUE
Washington, DC
Fifth Year Thesis. Student: Abdul Muziker; Critic: Samir Younés

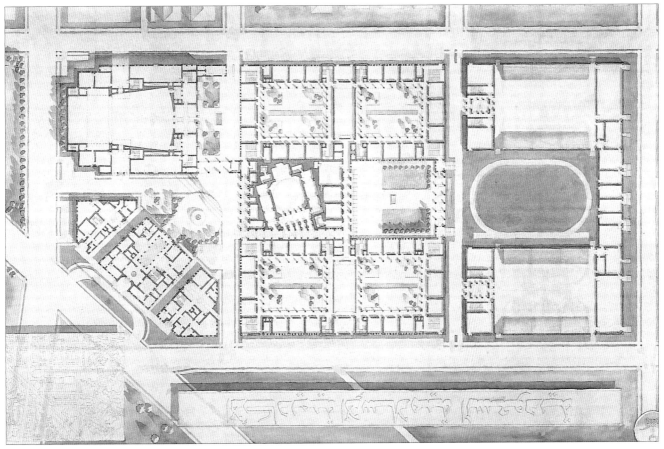

Sacred Buildings

HALL CHURCH AND BAPTISTERY

Sauvie Island, Oregon

Graduate Thesis. Student: Duncan McRoberts; Critics: Cara Carroccia, Richard Economakis

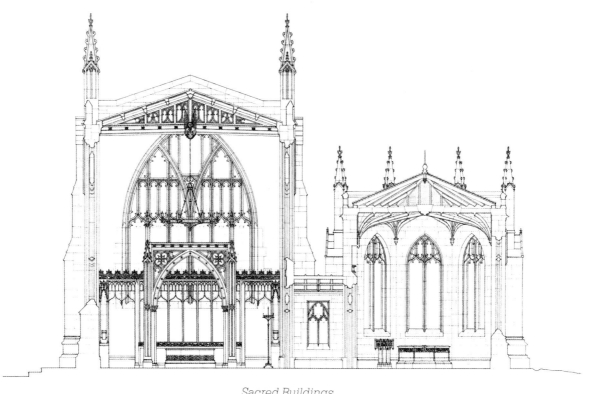

Sacred Buildings

REDEVELOPMENT OF CAPITOL AVENUE
Washington, DC
Fourth Year Studio. Student: Mark Gage; Critic: Duncan Stroik

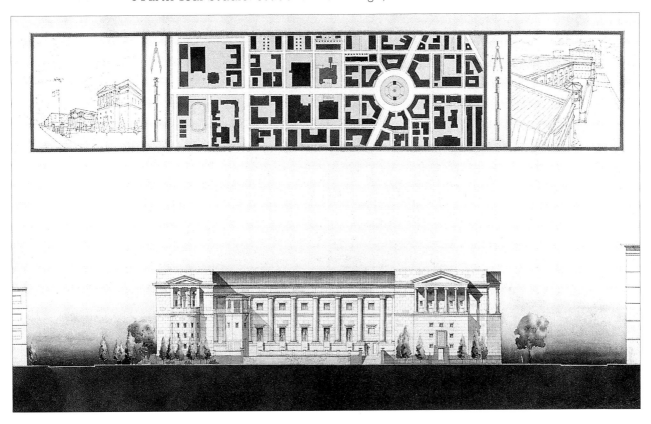

RECONSTRUCTION OF THE BORGO VATICANO
Rome, Italy
David Mayernik, Architect

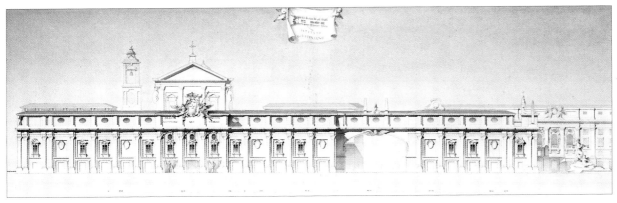

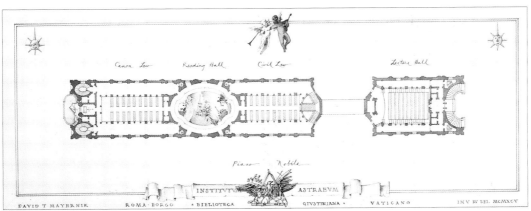

Blocks and Streets

RICHMOND RIVERSIDE
Richmond on Thames, England
Quinlan Terry, Architect

ROOSEVELT ROAD
Chicago, Illinois
DLK Architecture

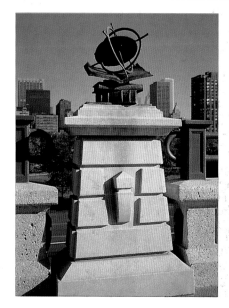

CENTER FOR CULTURAL AND RELIGIOUS STUDIES
Miyajima, Japan
Fifth Year Competition Studio. Students: H Jules Dingle, Frank Fu-Jen Yang; Critic: Michael Lykoudis

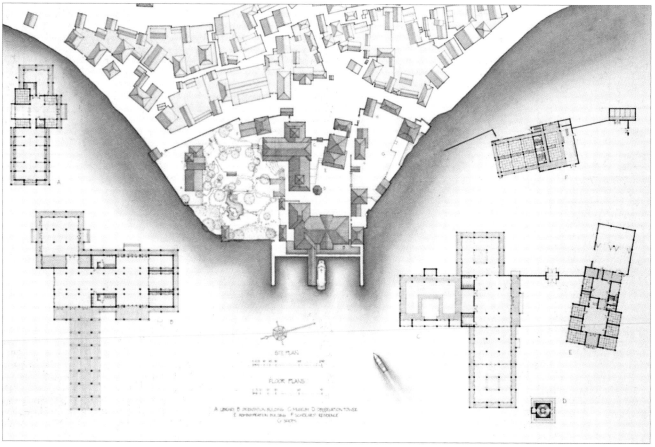

POUNDBURY
Dorchester, England
Deupi–Economakis Design Partnership

Blocks and Streets

LE PLESSIS ROBINSON
Affordable Housing and Center for the Cognitively Disabled; Paris, France
Marc and Nada Breitman, Architects

Blocks and Streets

BRIDGE BETWEEN GREECE AND TURKEY

Richard Economakis and Baki Sukan, Architects

UPPER MARKET MONUMENT
Augusta, Georgia
David Colgan, Architect

Public Spaces and Monuments

MONUMENT TO JOSEPH BECK
Luxemburg
Léon Krier, Architect

sculpture by Robert Krier

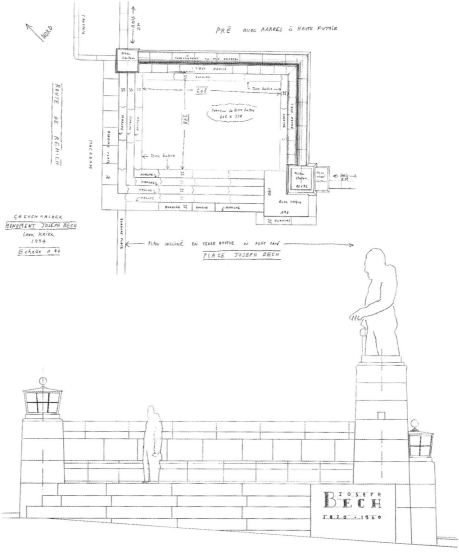

DESIGN FOR A NATIONAL GARDEN
Washington, DC
Victor Deupi

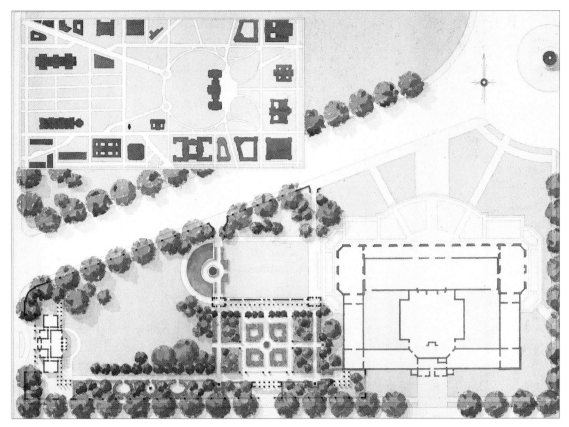

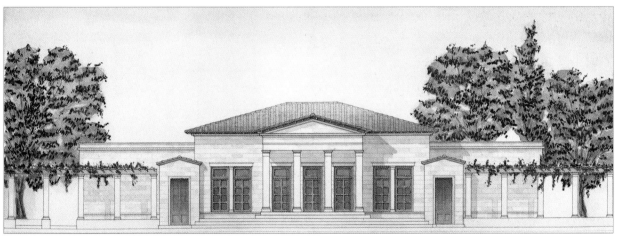

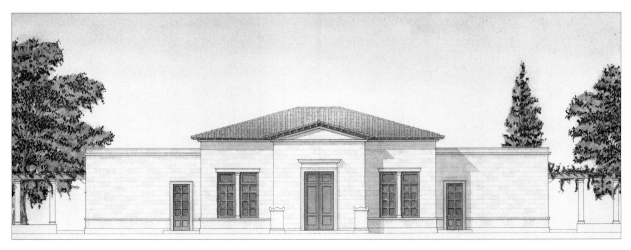

BRICKELL AVENUE BRIDGE
Miami, Florida
Jorge Hernandez, Architect

CEMETERY FOR THE CITY OF ROME

Rome Graduate Studio. Student: Robert Pilla; Critic: Victor Deupi

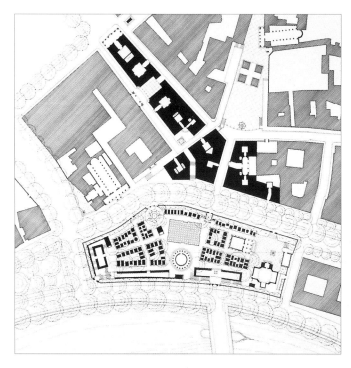

THREE PROPOSALS FOR THE CITY OF ROME

Rome Graduate Studio. H Wang, W Feng, C Carpella, P Dodd, M Kinasiewicz, J Onyango

Hai Wang

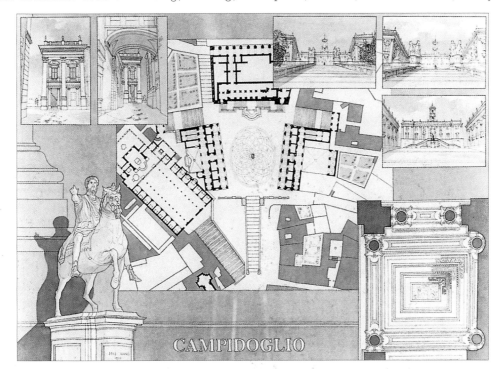

Weiqing Feng

Carmine Carpella
Philip Dodd
Weiqing Feng
Michelle Kinasiewicz
John Onyango
Hai Wang

Public Spaces and Monuments

RECONSTRUCTION OF BEIRUT
Lebanon
Samir Younés, Architect

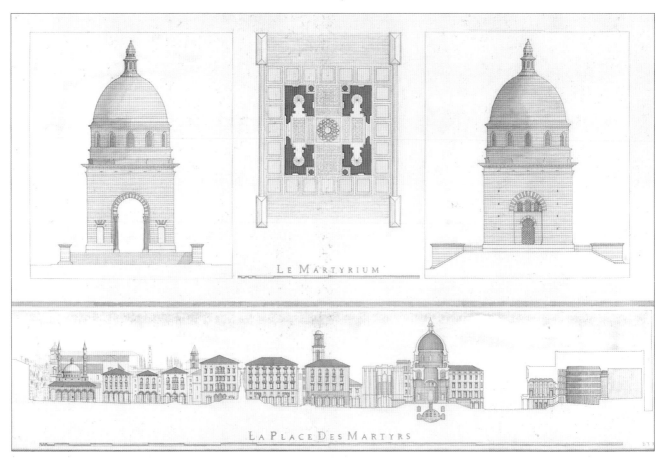

LE MARTYRIUM

LA PLACE DES MARTYRS

Quarters and Neighborhoods

BRUAY-LA-BUISSIERE
Urban Restructuring of the Town of Nouveau Monde, France
Marc and Nada Breitman, Architects

Quarters and Neighborhoods

CENTER FOR CLASSICAL STUDIES
Nisyros, Greece
Richard Economakis

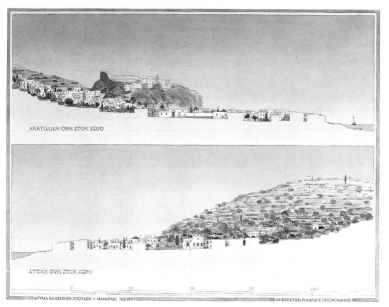

ΑΝΑΤΟΛΙΚΗ ΟΨΗ ΣΤΟΝ ΧΩΡΟ

ΔΥΤΙΚΗ ΟΨΗ ΣΤΟΝ ΧΩΡΟ

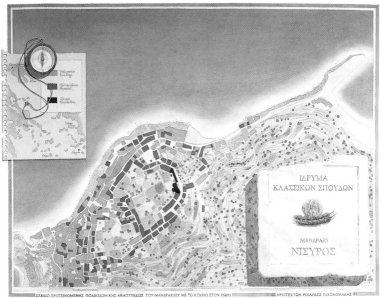

ΙΔΡΥΜΑ ΚΛΑΣΣΙΚΩΝ ΣΠΟΥΔΩΝ

ΜΑΝΔΡΑΚΙ ΝΙΣΥΡΟΣ

ΑΝΑΤΟΛΙΚΗ ΟΨΗ

ΔΥΤΙΚΗ ΟΨΗ

Quarters and Neighborhoods

MASTER PLAN COMPETITION
Plainfield, Illinois
Fourth Year Competition Studio. Students: R Arosemena, T McManus, D Samora, M A Soundy; Critic: N Crowe

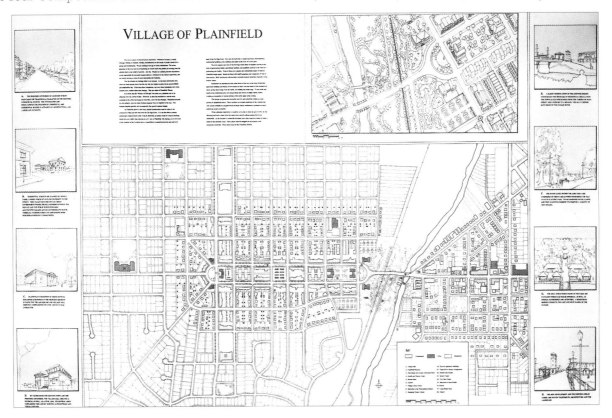

CHANNAHON TOWN CENTER COMPETITION

Norman Crowe, Architect

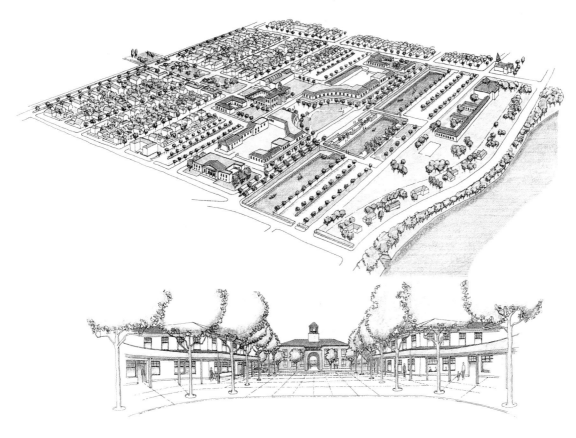

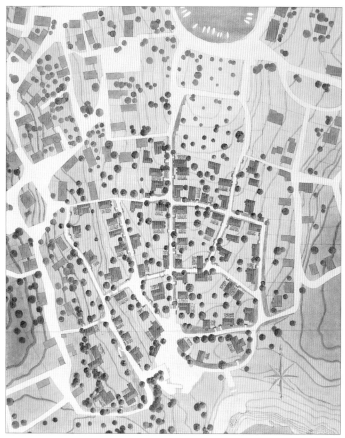

PITIOUSA
Spetses, Greece
Porphyrios Associates

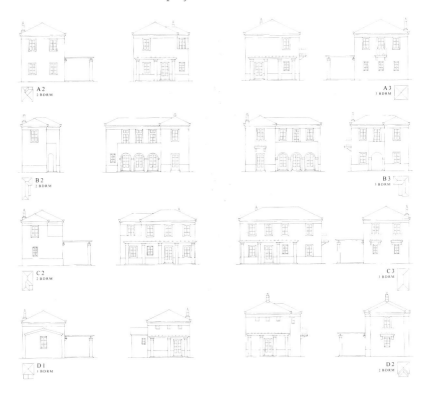

MASTER PLAN FOR NAUPLION, GREECE
Summer School Program in Architecture and Urban Design
Students: R Arosemena, A Bajuyo, J C Bohorquez, M Cifuentes, V Cordero-Rappl, E Deegan, P Goudet, W Liang, W J Park,
A A Ishizaki, K Raspanti, M A Soundy, L Schmitt; Critics: R Economakis, M Lykoudis. Teaching Assistant: S Papadopoulos

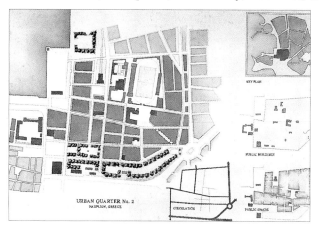

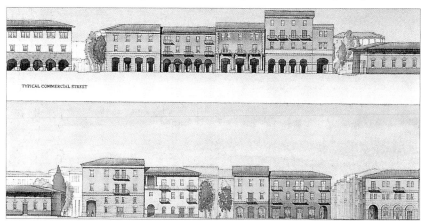

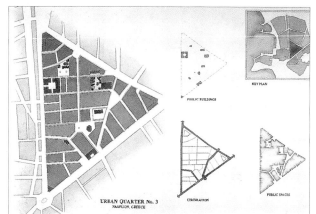

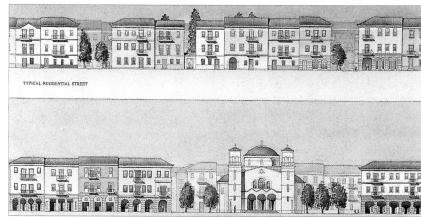

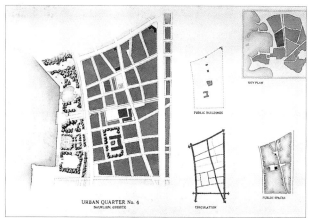

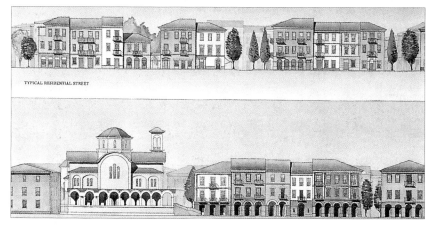

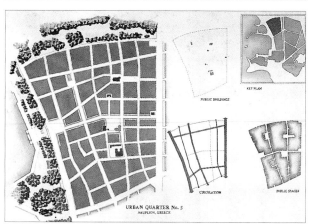

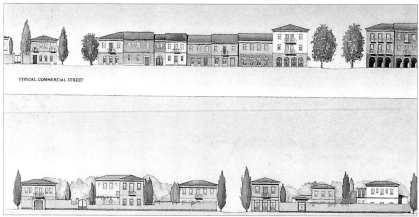

Cities, Towns, and Villages

HAYMOUNT
Virginia
John Clark, Developer

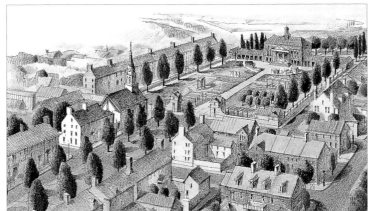

NEW OLYMPIA TOWN PLAN
A Proposal for a Permanent Site for Olympian Games
Graduate Thesis. Students: Edward Deegan, Thomas Marano; Critics: Norman Crowe, Richard Economakis

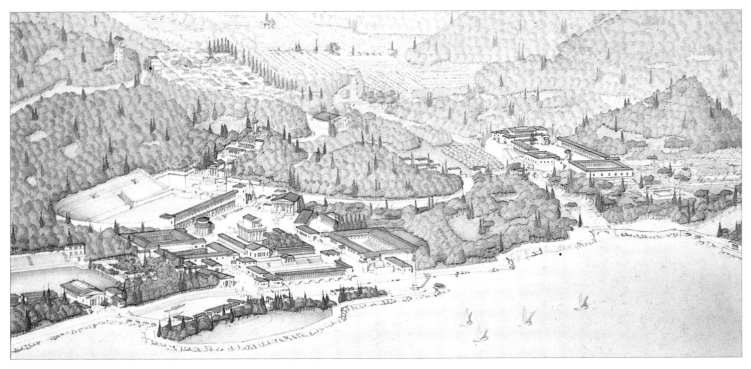

MASTER PLAN AND URBAN DESIGN
South Bend, Indiana
Design Team: Charles Beck, Michael Mesko, Michael Lykoudis, Sean Nohelty, Tomas Ramirez, Lisa Schmitt

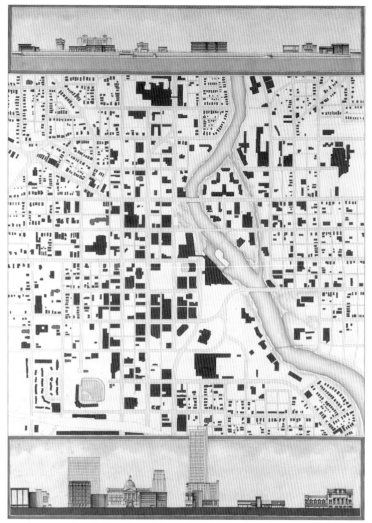

Existing

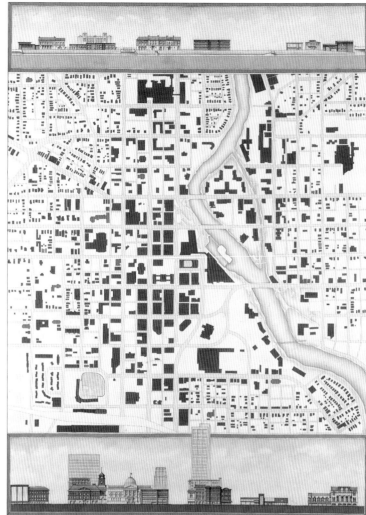

10-Year Plan

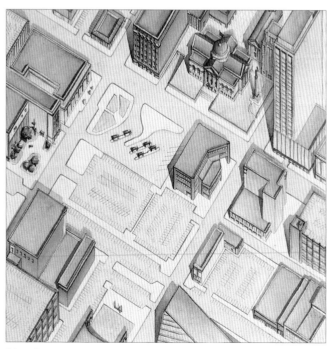

Main Square: Existing

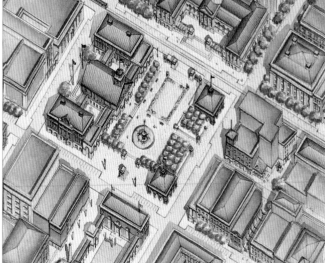

Main Square: Proposed, 2075

Cities, Towns, and Villages

35-Year Plan

80-Year Plan

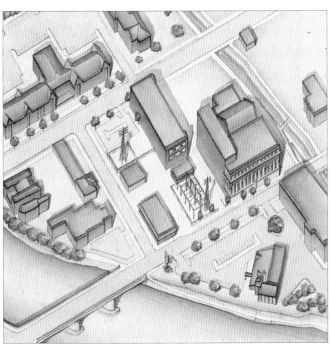

East Race Island: Existing

East Race Island: Proposed, 2075

Cities, Towns, and Villages

A MOST FORMIDABLE TASK
Samir Younés

'Everywhere we remain unfree and chained to technology, whether we passionately affirm or deny it. But we are delivered to it in the worst possible way when we regard it as something neutral; for this conception of it, to which today we particularly like to do homage, makes us utterly blind to the essence of technology.'
M Heidegger

Future historians will undoubtedly emphasize certain powerful acts of will, expressed in key international conferences which strongly marked contemporary thought on the city. These are: Rational Architecture of 1975; the Declarations of Palermo of 1978, and of Brussels of 1980; A Vision of Europe and the Conference of Emerging Classical Architects of 1992; the Art of Building Cities held in Chicago in 1995; and Urban Renaissance, which convened in Bologna in 1996. These conferences have demonstrated that the knowledge needed for the reconstruction of the city has to a large extent been acquired and that there is no longer a sense of alarming urgency to recuperate a view which is devoid of the tenets of modernism. The reconstruction of the city is no longer the object of a desire which is experienced as an absence, for it is being thought and built. However, the reconstruction of the city still remains an incomplete project, for a major obstacle prevents its realization. This obstacle is *technique*.

Technique, according to the late Jacques Ellul, denotes the pursuit of utmost rationality and efficiency of means that can be attained at a given time. It seeks to organize all facets of human activities towards maximal efficiency. As such, it is characterized by its concrete applications, and more importantly by an intentionality which addresses the totality of utilized means. While the machine is the most obvious manifestation of the domain of technique, it is only one among its many phenomena. Thus, technique may be seen to include the bureaucracy of a government which has become a thing in itself, rather than the accomplishments it is supposed to implement, such as the contemporary practice of city planning. Another example might include the intervention of media technologies in the quality and distribution of knowledge. Technique also designates the object, the technological phenomenon itself – for example, the computer – whereas technology designates a discourse on technique –

for example, computer science. In this sense the use of the two terms, technology and technique, can be clarified by saying that the relation between technology and technique is analogous to that between physiology and the body.[1]

Now, what interests us presently is the major qualitative shift of technique in the decades following the Second World War. Technological development ceased to be linear, rigid, monovalent, and based on the old division of labour. Instead it became flexible, polyvalent, and applied universally at a scale never before attained. More importantly, the ensemble of complementary elements that compose technique reached such a high degree of interdependency and inter-correlation that they now formed a system: a technological system.[2] Thus, any change in one of these elements invariably entails repercussions on all the others, because they are organized in terms of one another. These elements in turn gain their greater significance by virtue of the place that they occupy within the system and their favored intrinsic relationships over other relationships. Consider, for example, the inter-relationship between the building industry, the timber industry, and steel manufacturing; the automobile industry, and the highway, rail, and air-traffic network; nature conservancy laws, employment, and political practices.

The technological system came to be characterized by: autonomy, automatism, self-expansion, universality, causal progression and an absence of finality.[3] In short, the technological system developed a powerful determinism, with its own laws: a reality *in se*. It became monistic. Now, whereas this list is not exhaustive or closed, it accounts for the system's dual directionality. On the one hand, its integrated functions make it autonomous, and on the other, its external relationships form an integrating, all-inclusive function. This means that the technological system operates on the basis of its internal logic alone. Thus, the technological system drastically alters any area which it enters while remaining relatively unchanged. A comparative examination of the nature, quality, and operations of an architectural firm, before and after the introduction of the computer, will demonstrate that it was architects who had to change and adapt to a considerable extent to fit the computer's dictates, rather than the reverse. But what is more important to note is the work of architects who, without actually using a computer, still produce buildings which could have been produced by a computer. Such is the extent of their immersion in the technological system.

The technological system engenders a distinct mentality which organizes everything into processes and applications. Thus, one must use economic planning to deal with an economy, city planning to deal with the city, and long-range planning to conceive of buildings able to accommodate any future expansion. All are technologies; and throughout these processes, technological growth refers to itself, replicates and resembles itself, in a causal progression and with an absence of finality. The vicious circularity of these developments recalls the Hegelian 'spurious infinity',[4] and this is the reason why growth and development are confused in the technological system, engendering, for example, the severe problems of scale in cities and buildings.

The contemporary city grows by incessant annexation of land around its periphery, transforming previous natural territory into a conglomeration of monofunctional zones.[5] These zones attain such a size that it becomes imperative to build the countless highways and automobiles needed for vast displacement of people, necessitating more mining, fuel, metals, plastics, and specialists. With the increase of zones, there is an increase in highways; with the increase of highways, there is an increase in automobiles; with the increase of automobiles, there is an ever larger need for parking lots; and as more and more parking lots are needed, more and more buildings and city blocks are removed to make space for them . . . This is a spurious infinity in the sense of continual external and internal growth, asymptotically approaching but never reaching closure, while furthering the illusion that the infinite will be attained if one had but one more fact. Thus are the infinite and the indeterminate confused.

Considerable problems arise when the idea of infinity, as developed by the sciences and an abstract technological will, invades the fine arts and explodes the clear boundaries between them, to the point where their very identity is put in question. This precipitates the most pervasive fracture in the very idea of making in art, because that which characterizes the maker: creativity, invention, genius, comes to be considered as the logical opposite of that which governs the made: imitation, rules, conventions. Furthermore, when the means of art tend toward an infinity, then art's nature and ends are eclipsed, and the artistically true and the artistically real collapse into each other.

This explains the rabid confusion on the part of modernist artists and architects, who assume that a change in means necessarily entails a change in ends. In other words, the means of individuating a work of art have come to be confused with the reasons for individuating, as well as the purposive finality towards which this individuating tends. Clearly, the presence of the spurious infinity is tied causally to the contemporary notion of progress and the lack of feedback which characterize an ever expanding technological system.[6]

Whereas the spurious infinity is only one characteristic of technique, it nevertheless serves to point to some of technique's far reaching consequences. First, technique is not a neutral tool which we can use or discard as we please, for human freedom in the technological milieu has a strong technological directionality. Much of what surrounds us, since infancy, is a technology of sorts, as education and propaganda technologies are simultaneously employed toward making us fit this milieu, either by adapting us or by breaking any resistance which we might have. Hence Jean Baudrillard's claim that an individual in a technological society is only free as a consumer.[7] Indeed, even the most general reflection on the measure of our freedom within the technological milieu leads to the conclusion that this milieu greatly facilitates freedom, as long as the means and the products employed fit within a technological framework. When new technologies cause unemployment, the technological milieu hastens to institute new technologies, such as retraining facilities, job placement centres and psychological clinics designed to help cope with the loss of a livelihood.

Thus a problem's cause and the compensation for it are both technologically mediated,[8] and consequently, humanity's ability to acquire a point of view about cause and effect in the technological milieu is seriously impaired. As a result of this, freedom is impaired.

The protagonists of technology usually laud its 'liberating and democratizing' effects on widening the possibilities of choice in the vast world of consumption, thereby confusing technological criteria with democratic criteria, as if it was the norm for every new technological product to be accompanied with the possibility to judge its value, modify it, and perhaps reject it if need be. But, more importantly, as both Ellul and Baudrillard remarked: the multiplication of consumer choices is certainly not a measure of human freedom. And ethical concerns or political will, for that matter, have proven to have little effect, as they are unnecessary for technological growth. For example, televisions and automobiles *will* be produced irrespective of one's position as to their effects on learning habits or atmospheric pollution. For, with regard to technological production, human actions are restricted to one of two choices: either to choose between various television or automobile manufacturers, in which case there is considerable flexibility and freedom, or to resist consuming them, in which case the best that can be achieved is a slowing down of a certain production.

Human action, in the final analysis, can only influence the rate of speed of technological production. Technique here presents itself as a contingent inescapability. Such a realization, which led Ellul to distinguish between *kinds* of choice, based on ethical considerations, and *zones* of choice,[9] which are dictated by the technological system, led to Léon Krier's demand that in a genuinely pluralist world we be allowed the choice between living in a traditional city or a modernist zone.[10]

While the technological milieu does not eliminate the natural and social milieux, it nevertheless intervenes by preventing or by seriously disrupting the autonomy that they previously enjoyed. Here are three examples. One, the technological system – inside the technological milieu – integrates through fragmentation: that is, it reduces and separates the various elements that used to constitute any given entity, a system, until it no longer functions as such. This point is clearly illustrated by the technological system's disruption of the ecosystem, and by the city's fragmentation into monofunctional zones. Each fragment is isolated, treated, and compartmentalized according to a specific set of parameters which are relevant only to the rationality and efficiency of the technological system. Accordingly, an urban area comes to signify a certain tax revenue and monetary value, forming a certain percentage of an economic projection. Therefore, anything that becomes integrated within the technological system assumes and reflects its characteristics, and the whole is consequently treated as a reality.

Second, if we compare the kind of mediation which characterizes the natural and social milieux, at least up to the early nineteenth century, with the mediation which characterizes the technological milieu, we can see that the former is eliminated or at least de-signified.[11] Consider the entire rubric of thought which could be grouped under symbolization as mediation; for example, myth, *poesis*, and *mimesis*, as ways to symbolize the world and mediate between a universal and a particular. In this view meaning is both immanent and transcendent; it is never confined to an internal relationship alone. Architecture, the tool, the symbol, and the word have form and receive their meaning from alluding to a truth, to a reality; and their manifestations involve all the dialectical tensions between a consciousness, an experience, and an object. Meaning here points to several directions at once, and making (Greek ποειν, *poesis*; Latin *facere*) always has a purpose which is distinctly other than itself or its own processes. For example, tectonics alludes at once to a mythopoeic function and to construction.

But technique operates on the principle of non-contradiction, where the correspondence between things, if it is not to be contradictory, must be one of specific identity. It is qualified by an overriding internal logic which excludes tensions. As such, technique is non-dialectical because meaning is always confined to an internal relationship. This is the reign of immanence, characterized by an opacity toward external meaning.[12] Note, for example, the contradiction inherent in the phrase: architecture of industrial references. This architecture hardly refers to technique. It *is* technique; it sought and attained an identity with technique by becoming both its instrument and expression. Hence, the distance needed for symbolization as mediation has been eliminated.[13] Meaning collapsed and with it the possibility of having a *sensus communis*, the very basis upon which cities and civic structures rest their foundations. This is so because making, in the technological milieu, always resembles itself and replicates itself; it is its own ends: a spurious infinity.

With similar interventions, technique imposed itself as the sole mediator, the *sine qua non* for the apprehension of reality, the relations between nations, among individuals and between individuals and various technologies. Consider, for example, the large role played by the mass media in propagating consumption[14] and shaping appetites for technological products. Note how with each demand for the satisfaction of these appetites, an ever greater dependency on technique comes to permeate the totality of social relations. From this level, technique passes from being the sole mediator between humanity and the natural and social milieux, to intensify the immediacy of its conditioning of experience. Thus, nothing stands between humanity and technique.

Third, technique truly acts as a barrier between us and other milieux. Nature, for example, is increasingly remote and our access to it is almost totally dependent on technological means. Those interested in finding a forest must rely inescapably on technological means; and once there they will invariably be accompanied by the gadgets with which the technological milieu abounds: cellular telephones, portable televisions, and computers. The much heralded Super-Information Highway is the clearest demonstration of the supreme saturation of physical reality by the technological system. In this case, technique will finally fill the realm of the concrete, which it defines as the real. This led Ellul to exclaim that: 'Ultimately, the "ideal" for this new environment, is to exist to such a degree that nothing else exists.'[15]

As an ultimate form of mediation, technique has become an ultimate common measure on the individual, societal, and natural levels. This leads to the most troublesome conclusion that technique enframes – Heidegger's *Gestell* – reality and enframes the possible. The reality to which humanity in the technological milieu is supposed to refer is abstracted from its social milieu, and given as an 'already there'; for example, the consumption-oriented society as an 'already there'. And technique established itself as a reality by virtue of its filling the world with a myriad of cybernetically diffused images, thus acquiring a pseudo-omnipresence; a point commonly stressed by Ellul and Heidegger.[16]

In technique's world, objects are designed to last but a short period of time and replace each other at vertiginous speed. Yet, because of this proliferation, the object recedes to an unimportant position, while significance resides in the multiplication of means. The means have come to be regarded as permanent while the object is now utterly contingent. Thus, the proliferation of objects appears less significant a phenomenon, only because the means make it possible. This is an enframing of the real, where both a trivialized subject and an obsolete object become subservient to the means. The concrete is occupied by a set of technological products, while the technological system as an invisible intentionality enframes the limits of the possible. Here, the real is defined as the concrete, the factual; and what is possible is defined as that which is *technologically possible*. Meaning in the phenomenal world of technique is reduced

to its concrete appearance alone, a nominalism.

This technologically determined reality reduces essence to appearance, and the confusion of the two implies a rejection of the categorical distinction drawn by Wittgenstein between 'seeing' and 'seeing as'. Here, the distinction between the representation and the productions of aesthetic culture on the one hand, and technological productions on the other, has collapsed. This explains why those whose thought has been formed by the technological order can only consider the reconstruction of traditional architecture and the city as a re-enactment, and cannot fathom its paradigmatic value and contemporary applicability; because to confuse 'seeing' with 'seeing as' means a confusion as to the nature, means and ends of artifice, and ultimately a confusion between the artistically true and the artistically real. This explains much of the contemporary refusal of any transcendent reality which instantiates the characteristics of a given phenomenon. Therefore, the relationship of a universal to a particular, of an enduring to a contingent, of a type to a building, is repressed as technique attempts to replace the enduring.

It must be affirmed, once again, that despite the fact that visible reality is occupied by technological phenomena, technique itself stands outside, as an all-encompassing envelope around nature and society, capable of effecting changes and determining directions. And the acceptance of such an idea entails an *a priori* and unconscious consent to technique's considerable reduction of our freedom. But although technique tends in the direction of a narrow determinism, its dominion is not complete and should be rejected. This rejection, however, entails neither passing an indiscriminate judgment on anything technological, nor a simplistic technophobic confrontation between humans and machines; for the machine, as mentioned earlier, is but one of many aspects of technique. Nor should it be assumed that the mere analysis of the daunting obstacles posed by technique suffices for their removal.

We never forget how technological production duplicated, competed with, and eventually displaced art and architectural production. Such an intervention collapsed the distance between the productions of aesthetic culture and technological production, followed by a cybernetic diffusion of technique which caused the erosion of boundaries between various arts. Thus, to simply demand that architecture and the city be dissociated from technological production is hardly sufficient. We have to reflect on the matter from a position which is outside the empire of technique. For this purpose we need to work on building the distance from technique, in view of facilitating a standpoint, a sense of composure and a point of view *vis-à-vis* culture. Technique's hegemony is not an irreversible event in history. Indeed, the most cursory reflection on the technological milieu reveals that, despite massive efforts, we are not totally adapted to it. We recall here Ellul's analogy that if one is traveling on a train one cannot see the direction the train is taking. One must therefore disembark from the train of technique in order to gain a perspective on it, and realize decisions which are out-side of it, in the hope of putting it in its place as just one of many available means. If we succeed in firmly securing this standpoint, then the mythopoeic function, the paradigm, and the reconstruction of the city could progress relatively unimpeded. Of course, they were always there, only we could not see beyond the opaque veil of technique. To rend this veil is our next project. A most formidable task.

Notes

1 The work of Jacques Ellul is an invaluable reference for these clarifications. See the preface of his *La technique ou l'enjeu du siècle*, A Colin (Paris), 1954, and his *Perspectives on our Age*, J Neugroschel (trans), Seabury Press (New York), 1981, pp33.

2 The passage from industrialization to the emergence of the technological system is lucidly analyzed in J Ellul, *Le système technicien*, Calmann-Lévy (Paris), 1977.

3 See J Ellul, ibid, Chapters 5–12 , where these characteristics are thoroughly analyzed. See also, G Hottois, *Le signe et le technique*, Aubier (Paris), 1984.

4 I am indebted to David Lovekin for this reference on Hegel. See G W F Hegel, *Hegel's Science of Logic*, A W Miller (trans), Allen & Unwin (London), 1969. Book One, Chapter 2, pp137–50. See also Lovekin's *Technique, Discourse and Consciousness*, Lehigh University Press, 1991, p98–105.

5 Léon Krier in this respect has provided a powerful critique of contemporary zoning practices. See *Léon Krier: Architecture and Urban Design, 1967–1992*, R Economakis (ed), Academy Editions (London) 1992.

6 Consider, for example, how we continually pollute water and continually build the factories to purify this water.

7 J Baudrillard, *La société de consommation*, Gallimard (Paris), 1974.

8 J Ellul, *Le système technicien*, Chapter 4.

9 Ibid, Conclusion.

10 L Krier, 'Vers un pluralisme', in *Prix Européen de la Reconstruction de la Ville*, Archives d'Architecture Moderne (Brussels), 1987.

11 Mediation, here, designates that which serves as a vehicle for conveying ideas between two or more realms.

12 Compare, for instance, the hut and the maison domino. Note how the hut, as a type, allows for a distance between itself and the multitude of buildings of varied characters which it generates, as well as an indissociable unity of form and meaning, constituting architecture's artistic truth. The maison domino, on the other hand, can only replicate and resemble itself with no distance. In this mentality, structural form is dissociated from character and meaning, which become removable attributes, thus displacing the issue of artistic truth.

13 I do not share the opinion of some scholars who see *technique* as a kind of symbolic thought. But assuming this hypothesis for a moment, one must emphatically note that if technique were a symbolic form, then we certainly have privileged this one symbolic form to the near exclusion of other symbolic forms. Furthermore, we have used earlier symbolic forms to serve the ends of technique. Following Ellul, one sadly observes that in this century, and especially after the Second World War, humanity, and especially technologically advanced nations, have wagered everything on one game: technique.

14 See H M McLuhan, *Understanding Media: The Extensions of Man* (New York), 1964 .

15 J Ellul, op cit p46.

16 See J Ellul, *La parole humiliée*, Seuil (Paris), 1981; and M Heidegger, *The Question Concerning Technology*, Harper & Row (New York), 1977.